A Letter From the Co-Founders of Secondary Entrance

Dear Customer,

We're delighted that you've purchased a Secondary Entrance practice pack! Before you begin, we want to tell you about the story of Secondary Entrance, and what our ethos is when it comes to providing education services.

As of June 2017, we had both been privately tutoring students for multiple years, and at a coffee table conversation we realised that we shared a few common frustrations. Firstly, we felt that existing practice tests for 11+ students appeared to focus on coaching exam technique rather than training aptitude. Secondly, materials in the existing market seemed to be grossly overpriced, and money was increasingly becoming a factor in academics. We also both understand that it is only healthy for a child to work a limited number of hours in a day, and that it is therefore crucial to make the most out of every working minute. Lo and behold, Secondary Entrance was born.

We set a goal: to develop affordable new resources of the highest quality. Together, we recruited the best minds from top universities in the world to create training tests for the four main pillars of secondary school admission: maths, English, verbal reasoning and non-verbal reasoning. Every question has been hand-crafted, debated over and scrutinised to ensure that it meets our exceptionally high standards. We ensured that the papers liberally use graphics to help develop children's visual and spatial skills alongside their intellect. In total, we've produced resources that give your child every chance of gaining admission to the school of their choice.

While our papers educate as well as monitor, we know that there is no substitute to having a good teacher. As such, we decided to compile a portfolio of tutors to offer both in-person and online tuition. We personally interviewed a wide range of candidates, selected the very best and trained them to Secondary Entrance quality. To complete our offerings, we've also uploaded a range of free resources on www.Independent11Plus.co.uk that we're constantly building on. Whatever it is that you need, we want to make sure that we've got you and your child covered. We'd like to wish your child all the best in their academic endeavours, not only for their upcoming exams but also for the journey that follows.

Warmest regards and happy testing,

Founders of Secondary Entrance
www.SecondaryEntrance.co.uk

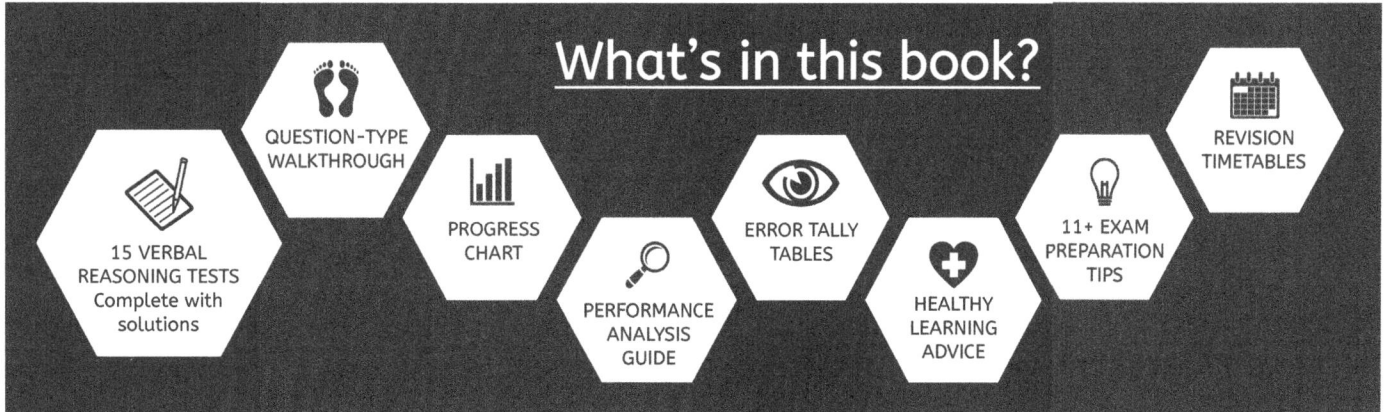

What's in this book?

- **15 VERBAL REASONING TESTS** Complete with solutions
- **QUESTION-TYPE WALKTHROUGH**
- **PROGRESS CHART**
- **PERFORMANCE ANALYSIS GUIDE**
- **ERROR TALLY TABLES**
- **HEALTHY LEARNING ADVICE**
- **11+ EXAM PREPARATION TIPS**
- **REVISION TIMETABLES**

What makes these books so special?

There are three core aspects to what makes our papers unique, and which allow us to best support your child:

Quality
We offer the highest quality 11+ practice papers on the market, suitable for independent schools.

Diversity
We have 240 varied 11+ papers across four subjects, and our content is highly enriched with graphics and visuals.

Flexibility
Our papers get harder from Book 1 to 4 in each subject, and are all also highly effective for general aptitude training.

11+ Practice Papers
For Independent Schools & Aptitude Training

Verbal Reasoning

Book 2

Orders: Please contact www.How2Become.com

ISBN: 9781912370788

First published in 2020 by How2Become Ltd.

Copyright © Secondary Entrance Ltd.

All rights reserved. Apart from any permitted use under UK copyright law, no part of this publication may be reproduced or transmitted in any form or by any means, electronic or mechanical, including photocopying, recording, or any information, storage or retrieval system, without permission in writing from the publisher or under licence from the Copyright Licensing Agency Limited. Further details of such licenses (for reprographic reproduction) may be obtained from the Copyright Licensing Agency Ltd, Saffron House, 6-10 Kirby Street, London EC1N 8TS.

Disclaimer
Every effort has been made to ensure that the information contained within this resource is accurate at the time of publication. How2Become Ltd are not responsible for anyone failing any part of any assessment or selection process as a result of the information contained within this resource. How2Become Ltd and their authors cannot accept any responsibility for any errors or omissions within this resource, however caused. No responsibility for loss or damage occasioned by any person acting, or refraining from action, as a result of the material in this publication can be accepted by How2Become Ltd.

How2Become Ltd its authors are not affiliated with any exam board, third-party service, or organisation and all guidance and advice provided is designed as an educational aid only.

The information within this resource does not represent the views of any third-party service or organisation.

Printed and bound by CPI Group (UK) Ltd, Croydon, CR0 4YY

As part of this resource, you are entitled to claim a 30-day free trial to our powerful online Independent 11+ Online Tuition Course…

GET FREE ACCESS NOW:

www.My11PlusCourse.co.uk

- ☑ 30+ Video Tuition Modules on Maths, English, Verbal Reasoning, and Non-Verbal Reasoning;
- ☑ 100s of interactive practice questions;
- ☑ Detailed answers to each question – ensure you can help your child learn how to pass each question type;
- ☑ Over 6 Hours of Tuition for Your Child;
- ☑ The only Independent School 11+ online tuition, practice, & mock-exam resource – from How2Become and Secondary Entrance;
- ☑ Try free for 30 days!

Contents

Verbal Reasoning Question Type-Ordered Walkthrough (Full Sample Test)	6-13
Verbal Reasoning Test 16	14-18
Verbal Reasoning Test 17	19-23
Verbal Reasoning Test 18	24-28
Verbal Reasoning Test 19	29-33
Verbal Reasoning Test 20	34-38
Verbal Reasoning Test 21	39-43
Verbal Reasoning Test 22	44-48
Verbal Reasoning Test 23	49-53
Verbal Reasoning Test 24	54-58
Verbal Reasoning Test 25	59-63
Verbal Reasoning Test 26	64-68
Verbal Reasoning Test 27	69-73
Verbal Reasoning Test 28	74-78
Verbal Reasoning Test 29	79-83
Verbal Reasoning Test 30	84-88
Answers (Tests 16-30)	89-92
Progress Chart	93
Performance Analysis Guide	94
Question Type-Ordered Error Tally Table	95
Healthy Learning Tips	96-97
11+ Exam Preparation Advice	98
Revision Timetables	99-100

Verbal Reasoning - Walkthrough

Sample test, ordered by question type, with worked solutions and tips

Instructions for Usage:

> Run through this guide before attempting any of the papers.
> Attempt all of the questions, then review the worked solutions given.
> After completing tests, use this syllabus guide to find out weak topics.
> You can best document weak topics in the error tally table.

Question Type-Ordered Walkthrough

1) **REMOVING SUBSET WORDS**

   Sample Question: 3 consecutive letters have been taken out of a word. Select which three letter word **has been omitted**, from the options. Write your answer below:

   The W____HOUSE was packed with so many boxes!

   A. LIP   B. BID   C. ARE   D. BAR   E. ONE

   Answer and Explanation: C, ARE. This type of question assesses your child's ability to understand the context of a sentence, and the spelling of particular words too. There are two ways to answer this question, based on the assessment of these two parts of verbal reasoning. One could infer from the context of the sentence that W__HOUSE is warehouse, as this is where boxes could be stored. If this fails, and you are unable to solve the question, look at the 5 options you are presented with: WLIPHOUSE, WBIDHOUSE, WAREHOUSE, WBARHOUSE and WONEHOUSE. Even if you may never have heard of the word warehouse, the other options simply do not make sense as words. Therefore, an educated guess would be to choose warehouse.

   Tips: Write out the 5 options to fill in the blank to get a view of the words. Sometimes the sentence will not be there to help you, and you may see the word just by itself, but if you are given context then use everything you've got.

   Now Try This Question: 3 consecutive letters have been taken out of a word. Select which three letter word **has been omitted**, from the options. Write your answer below:

   H____S

   A. NOT   B. EEL   C. YET   D. BIN   E. POT

   Answer: B, EEL

2) **DECIPHERING WORDS**

   Three consecutive letters are removed from the word in CAPITALS. From the options, find the missing letters to complete the sentence.
   Write your answer below:

   LHER jackets are still in fashion today!

   A. OSE
   B. IGH
   C. IHT
   D. ENT
   E. EAT

   Answer and Explanation: E, EAT. Out of LOSEHER, LIGHHER, LIHTHER, LENTHER and LEATHER, only LEATHER is a real word. Substitute all of the options in to see which works. These questions are often harder than 'Removing Subset Words', as many of the options create words that look real. However, these may be less off-putting as the three letter words in the other question type can be distracting.

   Tips: Write out every single option if you are struggling, and eliminate the options that do not look like words. See if one word stands out to you as something that you recognise, and be sure to use the context of the sentence given to try and provoke your memory.

   Now Try This Question: Three consecutive letters are removed from the word in CAPITALS. From the options, find the missing letters to complete the sentence.
   Write your answer below:

   As soon as he got the ball he VOLLD it into the net!

   A. EEE
   B. EDE
   C. EYE
   D. END
   E. EEP

   Answer: C

3) **REARRANGED WORDS**

   Sample Question: You are required to take one letter from the first word and move it to the second word, creating **two new words**. Write your answer below:

   WHERE SEAT

   Answer and Explanation: HERE SWEAT. This question assesses your child's ability to build new words, understand the similarities between words, and even break down words into their constituent parts. In this case, look at the first word, WHERE. Which letter can you take out to form a new word? Taking out W gives HERE, so this is one possibility. Taking out H gives WERE which is also a word. WHRE, WHEE, WHER are not words therefore we have W and H to add to the next word. Adding W gives SWEAT, which is a word. Trying to add H to any part of SEAT will not make a recognisable word, and so the answer is HERE and SWEAT.

   Tips: Being systematic and taking out one letter at a time from the first option, and trying to add it to the second ensures you try all possible combinations, and do not miss the answer. Some words may seem odd outside the context of a sentence, but you must have faith in your vocabulary! Remember that there will only ever be one correct option.

   Now Try This Question: You are required to take one letter from the first word and move it to the second word, creating **two new words**. Write your answer below:

   THOSE CUE

   Answer: HOSE CUTE

4) **INCOMPLETE WORDS**

   Sample Question: Write the letter that will complete the word in front of the brackets and begin the word after the brackets. The SAME letter must fit into BOTH sets of brackets. Write your answer below:

   tim (_) ach, can (_) asy

   Answer and Explanation: E. Answering these questions is actually quite easy! Simply go through the alphabet one letter at a time, until you find a letter that fits all 4 words. Try A. Tima and aach are not words. Move onto B. Timb and bach are not words either. Move through the alphabet until you reach E. Tim(e)ach, can(e)asy. This method ensures you do not miss a letter. You must remember to check that the letter works in both sets of brackets.

   Tips: You may just notice a letter that fits into both brackets immediately. If this is the case, then it is very convenient. However, when you go into the exam, you want to be sure you can get this question correct every time.

Verbal Reasoning

Question Type-Ordered Walkthrough

Having a method of running through the alphabet quickly will ensure that you never get this question wrong, as long as you are not careless!

Now Try This Question: Write the letter that will complete the word in front of the brackets and begin the word after the brackets. The SAME letter must fit into BOTH sets of brackets. Write your answer below:

gon (_) ate, han (_) ram

Answer: G. Gon(g)ate, han(g)ram

5) COMBINING WORDS

Sample Question: Find one word from each group that together makes one correctly spelt word. The letters must not be rearranged. The word from the first group must always be used first. Write your answer below:

I am (one, four, five) (child, teen, adult) years old.

- A. Onechild
- B. Fourchild
- C. Fourteen
- D. Oneadult
- E. Fiveteen

Answer and Explanation: C, Fourteen. This question tests your ability to bring together two words, to create a brand new compound word. Reading the sentence gives you a hint as to what the word could be. It gives you context: the sentence is talking about how old someone is. Therefore, you would want to look for a number. Out of your 5 options, fourteen is the only possible answer.

Tips: Whilst you may be able to use the context of the sentence to get you to your answer, you could also try an alternative approach. Cover the sentence and look at your 5 options. Which one looks like a word? Onechild? Fourchild? Oneadult? Fiveteen? These are most definitely not words, and therefore the correct answer is Fourteen.

Now Try This Question: Find one word from each group that together makes one correctly spelt word. The letters must not be rearranged. The word from the first group must always be used first. Write your answer below:

(stroll, run, jog) (way, route, path)

- A. Strollway
- B. Jogroute
- C. Runpath
- D. Strollroute
- E. Runway

Answer: E, Runway

6) COMMON WORD ASSOCIATIONS

Sample Question: The word in brackets is formed from the main word. Identify the pattern to work out the missing word from the options given. Write your answer below:

Catching (tin), diameter (ate), separate (?)

A. PET   B. RAT   C. PES   D. REP   E. PAT

Answer and Explanation: E, PAT. This question is assessing how to follow a pattern in the first two words, and apply it to the last word. From 'catching' the word 'tin' has been formed. The 3rd letter is 't', and 'in' are the 6th and 7th letters. This is the same for 'diameter', where the 3rd letter is 'a', and the 6th and 7th letters are 'te', forming 'ATE'. Here, for 'separate,' the answer would be 'PAT' by the same method.

Tips: Look at the first two words, and how the word in brackets was made from the word outside the brackets. It may be one chunk taken out of the word, or a certain pattern of letters. This will give you the method to solve the last, unknown bracket. When there are repeated letters in a word, keep track of which one you are working with.

Now Try This Question: In each case, the word in brackets is formed from the main word. Identify the pattern to work out the missing word from the options given. Write your answer below:

Sergeant (ran), provider (ode), pipeline (?)

A. LIP   B. NEP   C. PIN   D. PEL   E. PEEL

Answer: C

7) ALPHABET CODES

Sample Question: Work out the relationship between the word and the code to solve the code and write your answer below:

A B C D E F G H I J K L M N O P Q R S T U V W X Y Z

Your teachers organise a treasure hunt at your school.

They give you the following code to solve to find the treasure.

LOOP is to KMLL. What is the code for DRESS?

Answer and Explanation: CPBON. Use the code given within the question to formulated a method of finding the answer. LOOP is to KMLL. Look at the first letter from each word: L and K. From your alphabet you can see that you need to go one letter backwards from L to get to K. Now look at the second letters. O and M. From your alphabet, you can see you must move two letter backwards from O to get to M. Look at the third letters. O and L. This is 3 letters backwards from O. You should now be able to spot a pattern. For the first letter, you move one letter backwards. For the second letter you move two letters backwards and so on.

Now you must follow this same method for DRESS. Start with D. One letter backwards from D is C. Two letters backwards from R is P. Three letters backwards from E is B. Four letters backwards from S is O. Five letters backwards from S is N. Therefore, DRESS is converted to CPBON.
Tips: Be very methodical and do not assume that the

Verbal Reasoning

Question Type-Ordered Walkthrough

pattern used will be static for all letters, therefore make sure you convert ALL LETTERS before you move on to using the rules that you think you have determined. Some questions will ask you to DECODE answers, as below. Give it a go and see if you can solve it without help! It is best not to rush, but to take it slow and get it right the first time.

Now Try This Question: Work out the relationship between the word and the code to solve the code and write your answer below:

A B C D E F G H I J K L M N O P Q R S T U V W X Y Z

Your teachers organise a treasure hunt at your school. They give you the following code to solve to find the treasure.

LOOP is to KMLL. Decode the following: SUFNG

Answer: TWIRL

8) ALPHABET PUZZLES

Sample Question: Find the pair of letters that will complete the sentence in the best way. The alphabet is provided below to help you. Write your answer below:

A B C D E F G H I J K L M N O P Q R S T U V W X Y Z

CM is to AP as GT is to __?

Answer and Explanation: EW. Look at how the first two letters were transformed into the second two letters. CM to AP. Start with the first letter of each. C to A. As you can see from the alphabet above, go backwards two letters from C, to get A. Now look at the second letters. M to P. Move 3 letters forward to go from M to P. Now apply this to the letters GT. From G, two letters backwards is E. From T, three letters forward is W. Therefore your answer is EW.

Tips: This question is similar to the Alphabet Codes style of question, and therefore should be treated similarly. Work out a method for getting from CM to AP, and apply this to GT. Always have a systematic method in mind.

Now Try This Question: Find the numbers and letters that will complete the sentence in the best way. The alphabet is provided below to help you. Write your answer below:

A B C D E F G H I J K L M N O P Q R S T U V W X Y Z

1F2G is to 3H4J as 1M2N is to __?

Answer: 3O4Q

9) NUMBER CODES

Sample Question: In each set of numbers, the number in the brackets is related to the two numbers either side of it. Find this relation to work out the missing number '(?)' in the third set. Choose one of the option and write your answer below:

Example:

Q: 4 (6) 2, 12 (14) 2, 7 (?) 4
A: (?) = 11

Question:

18 (2) 6, 56 (6) 8, 66 (?) 6

A. 11   B. 15   C. 12   D. 10   E. 21

Answer and Explanation: D, 10. Look at the first group of 3 numbers: 18 (2) 6. Look for a pattern connecting the two numbers outside to the one inside. Think of multiplication, division, addition and subtraction. If you are not sure, move onto the second group. 56 (6) 8. Looking at the first group, you may notice that 18 divided by 6 is 3. This number is one more than the number in the brackets, 2. The same method also fits with the second group. 56 divided by 8 is 7. This number is one more that the number in brackets, 6. For the last group, 66 divided by 6 is 11. 11-1 = 10. This means that your answer is D, 10.

Tips: This question relies on you spotting mathematical patterns, again by applying your 4 mathematical pillars: multiplication, division, addition and subtraction. If you are stuck trying to spot a pattern, try all of these individually. If you cannot solve it still, try combining a mix of 2 or more together to target those more challenging questions.

Now Try This Question: In each set of numbers, the number in the brackets is related to the two numbers either side of it. Find this relation to work out the missing number '(?)' in the third set. Choose one of the options and write your answer below:

Question:

12 (19) 4, 7 (15) 5, 8 (?) 1

A. 17   B. 5   C. 12   D. 25   E. 9

Answer: C

10) WORD RELATIONS

Sample Question: Select the two words inside the brackets that are connected in some way to the words outside the brackets. Write your answer below:

Ryan only likes certain types of boats. He likes the SPEEDBOAT, YACHT (canoe, bicycle, car, dinghy, plane) and many more.

Answer and Explanation: Canoe and Dinghy. This question tests your ability to identify patterns between groups of words. Here, the question has helped you, but this will not always be the case. You know that Ryan only likes certain types of boats. Two types are speedboats and yachts. From the 5 options, which of the others could also be types of boats? A canoe? Yes. A bicycle, car or plane? Most definitely not. Even if you do not know what a dinghy is, logically it should be the other option, since none of the others make sense. Therefore, your answer would be canoe and dinghy.

Tips: Some questions will not give you a hint at the beginning, and you will need to identify a pattern between the first two words outside the brackets without further context. Read the 5 options, and cross out ones that either mean the opposite or simply do not fit the pattern.

Verbal Reasoning

Question Type-Ordered Walkthrough

Now Try This Question: Select the two words inside the brackets that are connected in some way to the words outside the brackets. Write your answer below:

HURRY RUSH (slow, urgent, haste, carry, hinder)

Answer: Urgent and Haste

11) <u>SIMILES</u>

Select the word from the brackets that will complete the sentence in the most sensible way.
Write your answer below:

Open is to SHOW as close is to (door, lock, hide)

Answer and Explanation: Hide. These questions test your ability to understand the relationships between different words. To get to the answer, you need to understand how open relates to show, how open relates to close, and how show relates to a word in the brackets. Open and close are opposites, and so we are looking for the opposite of show, which is hide. Additionally, when you open something, you show the contents of it. Likewise, when you close something, you hide the contents of it.

Tips: Many students only look at the association between the first words (open and show, here) and then try to apply that to the second part of the sentence. You should instead look at the connections between all of the words, as described in the explainer above. Remember that there are two ways of getting to the answer. Often the words in the brackets may be similar, as is the case here wherein lock and hide are along the same lines. You should use both comparisons (eg. open to show as well as open to close) to figure out the best answer. These questions are dependent on having a good vocabulary, so get training!

Now Try This Question: Select the word from the brackets that will complete the sentence in the most sensible way.
Write your answer below:

Secret is to HIDE as disclose is to (reveal, shut, tale)

Answer: Reveal

12) <u>LETTER SEQUENCES</u>

Sample Question: Find the pair of letters that will continue the series. The alphabet is provided below to help you. Write your answer below:

A B C D E F G H I J K L M N O P Q R S T U V W X Y Z

UF, XH, AJ, DL, GN, ___?

Answer and Explanation: JP. This is a letter sequence, therefore the letters all follow a particular pattern. Look at the first letter of each part of the sequence. U --> X --> A --> D --> G. Next, look at the alphabet and you will notice that there are 2 letters between each of the terms: U (VW) X (YZ) A (BC) D (EF) G (HI) J. Using this method we have found the first letter of our answer, J.

Now look at the last letter of each part of the sequence. F --> H --> J --> L --> N. Using the same technique as before, look for a pattern connecting all these letters: F (G) H (I) J (K) L (M) N (O) P. We have found the second part of our answer, P. Our answer is therefore JP.

Tips: For these questions, it often helps to split the two letters of each term of the sequence, and try to work out the pattern of the first letters together, and then the second letters together. However, sometimes you will need to look at them as a whole to gain a proper understanding of what is happening. As for all puzzles that require you to study the alphabet, you should not worry about taking your time as it's important to make sure that you get it correct the first time round. Being one letter away from the correct answer means that you don't get the mark. It is often helpful to draw small loops between the letters when counting to help keep track.

Now Try This Question:

Sample Question: Find the pair of letters that will continue the series. The alphabet is provided below to help you. Write your answer below:

A B C D E F G H I J K L M N O P Q R S T U V W X Y Z

FT, CV, ZX, WZ, TB, ___?

Answer: QD

13) <u>NUMBER SEQUENCES</u>

Sample Question: Find the number that best complete the series. Fill in the missing blank with one of the following options and write your answer below:

2, 6, 18, ___, 162

A. 18   B. 34   C. 28   D. 54   E. 40

Answer and Explanation: D, 54. This is because between 2 and 6, there is a difference of 4. Between 6 and 18 there is also a difference of 12. It logically follows that the differences between the numbers in the sequence seem to be progressively tripling. 4 is multiplied by 3 to get 12. You can see that 12 x 3 = 36. Let us test to see if this works. 12 + 36 = 54. 36 x 3 = 108. 108 + 54 = 162, which is the final number in the sequence. We have confirmed that D, 54, is the correct answer.

Tips: Sequences act to test your child's ability to apply logic and identify patterns. Always think to yourself, what is the pattern between these numbers?

Use your four pillars of mathematics to help break down the problem if you are stuck.

- Addition
- Subtraction
- Multiplication
- Division

Do the sequences follow any of these patterns? If not, you could consider using square or cube numbers, or a combination of all of the above.

Now Try This Question: Find the number that best complete the series. Fill in the missing blank with one of the following options and write your answer below:

3, 4, 6, 10, 18, ___

A. 24   B. 30   C. 32   D. 34   E. 36

Answer: D

Verbal Reasoning

Question Type – Ordered Walkthrough

14) OPPOSITES

Sample Question: Select the pair of words, one from each group, that are **opposite in meaning** to each other, from the options given below. Write your answer below:

The opposite of (Little, Real, Thirsty) is (Tired, Hungry, Quenched).

- A. Little Tired
- B. Real Hungry
- C. Thirsty Hungry
- D. Thirsty Tired
- E. Thirsty Quenched

Answer and Explanation: E, Thirsty Quenched. This type of question tests your understanding of a particular word's definition, and how to apply this to work out words which mean the opposite. To begin, look at your first 3 words. The opposite of 'little' is big, which is not an option. The opposite of 'real' is unreal, which is also not an option. The opposite of 'thirsty' is something meaning not being thirsty. You may not know the word for this, but not being thirsty most definitely does not mean 'tired', or 'hungry'. Therefore, you are left with the word 'quenched', which does in fact mean the opposite of thirsty.

Tips: You may not know the meaning of all of the words you are presented with. Use logic and reasoning to try to find the best fit, and eliminate answers you know for sure are not correct. This way you learn from your mistakes, and build your vocabulary at the same time!

Now Try This Question: Select the pair of words, one from each group, that are **opposite in meaning** to each other, from the options given below. Write your answer below:

The opposite of (Onward, Jump, Together) is (Allow, Fight, Alone).

- A. Onward Allow
- B. Jump Fight
- C. Together Allow
- D. Together Alone
- E. Jump Alone

Answer: D

15) DIFFERENTIATING WORDS

Sample Question: Select the TWO odd words from the options given. Write your answer below:

Rain, Faint, Pain, Paint, Saint.

- A. Paint Faint
- B. Rain Pain
- C. Saint Paint
- D. Paint Rain
- E. Pain Saint

Answer and Explanation: B, Rain Pain. This question tests your ability to look at a group of words, and work out which two words do not fit in with the rest. They may be different in grammar, definition or just the pattern of letters. In this case, all the words end in either '-ain,' or '-aint'. 'Faint', 'Paint' and 'Saint'. Both 'Rain' and 'Pain' do not end in '-t', and so are the odd words in this case.

Tips: Remember that finding the odd words out may not just be on what they mean. Look for patterns in the letters, and the order of these letters too, especially if there is no obvious pattern as to what they mean. For example, they may all start or end with a certain letter.

Now Try This Question: Select the TWO odd words from the options given. Write your answer below:

Think, Query, Believe, Understand, Confuse, Acknowledge

- A. Think Confuse
- B. Believe Understand
- C. Confuse Believe
- D. Think Understand
- E. Query Confuse

Answer: E

16) VERBAL MATHS PROBLEMS

Sample Question: Choose the correct answer for the following problem. Write your answer below:

When a number is added to 34, the answer is 6 more than nine multiplied by four. What is the number?

A. 12   B. 6   C. 3   D. 8   E. 14

Answer and Explanation: D, 8. This question may seem odd in a Verbal Reasoning paper as it is maths, however, the ability to convert a question written in words into numbers is an important skill. In this case a number has been added to 34. The answer to this number is 6 more than 9 multiplied by 4. What sum can do you do straight away? 9 x 4 = 36. The answer to 6 more than this is 36 + 6 = 42. Which number, when added to 34 gives you 42? If you take 34 from 42 you will get the answer: 42 – 34 = 8.

Tips: Most students trip up when forming multiple sums, one after the other. Knowing how to create an equation takes practice - you should follow a logical manner and make sure that you check your answers at the end. Verbal Reasoning maths questions vary the sums and types of maths you need to use. However, they all have one thing in common: they require you to make a wordy question into a maths sum, so be sure to give this plenty of practice in advance of the exam!

Now Try This Question: Choose the correct answer for the following problem. Write your answer below:

When 15 is multiplied by a number, the answer is four less than when eight is multiplied by eight. What is the number?

A. 8   B. 3   C. 9   D. 2   E. 4

Answer: E

Verbal Reasoning

Question Type-Ordered Walkthrough

17) PRACTICAL MATHS PROBLEMS

Read the information provided and choose the single best answer for the question. Write your answer below:

5 friends decide to take part in a charity run. Harun runs 15 miles, whilst Aaron runs 2 miles less. Jacob runs 3 miles more than Aaron. Michael and Wenger both ran 1 more mile than Aaron. Who ran the most miles?

- A. Harun
- B. Aaron
- C. Jacob
- D. Michael
- E. Wenger

Answer and Explanation: C, Jacob. Harun runs 15 miles. Aaron runs 2 miles less than this, 15 - 2 = 13 miles. Jacob runs 3 miles more than Aaron, 13 + 3 = 16 miles. Michael and Wenger run 1 mile more than Aaron, 13 + 1 = 14 miles. The largest distance here is 16 miles, run by Jacob. This type of question tests your ability to understand a real life situation and solve a mathematical problem within this situation.

Tips: There will often be a lot of words which are conveying a relatively small amount of content. Try and filter out the core numbers here: 15, 2, 3 and 1, then figure out what sums you are going to be doing with them. Make sure to relate any calculated answers back to the individuals that they concern. If it helps, make a table with names and distances, when you calculate how far someone ran you can input this data in an organised way.

Now Try This Question: Read the information provided and choose the single best answer for the question. Write your answer below:

Megan, Julia and Amanda run a relay race. Amanda completed her part of the relay in 31 seconds. Julia finished her part 5 seconds quicker than Amanda, whilst Megan took 14 seconds longer than Amanda to complete her part. How long did the entire relay take?

- A. 60 seconds
- B. 102 seconds
- C. 50 seconds
- D. 81 seconds
- E. 73 seconds

Answer: C

18) FUNCTIONS

Sample Question: Choose the correct answer by completing the following equation with the correct sign as appropriate. Write your answer below:

$(560 \div 10 \times 2) \_\_ 2 = 8 \times 7 \div 1$

A. + B. - C. × D. ÷

Answer and Explanation: D, ÷. This is a BODMAS / BIDMAS style maths question. Head over to the Maths syllabus for more help on these types of questions. In this case, look at the brackets first: $(560 \div 10 \times 2)$. This is 112 as $560 \div 10 = 56$ and $56 \times 2 = 112$. Move over to the other side of the sum: $8 \times 7 \div 1 = 56$. Therefore 112 ? 2 = 56. We already know that 56×2 is 112, and so if you divide it by two, you would get 56 again. Therefore the answer is D, ÷.

Tips: These questions will continually test your understanding of BODMAS or BIDMAS, The Verbal Reasoning element is the ability to use symbols correctly. Furthermore, remember that letters can easily represent numbers, but that the laws of mathematics remain the same, so do not be phased by the presence of letters. You should treat them just as you would numbers. Many people find it helpful to rewrite the entire sum with brackets added in to clarify which sums are going to be done in which order.

Now Try This Question: Choose the correct answer by completing the following equation with the correct sign as appropriate. Write your answer below:

$93 + 3 \times 3 = (47 + 4) \times 4 \_\_ 2$

A. + B. - C. × D. ÷

Answer: D

19) ALGEBRAIC EQUATIONS

Using the provided code, complete the following sums writing your answer in **letters**:

$a = 5, b = 7, c = 3, d = 2, e = 8$

What is: $(a + b) \div (c \times d) = \_\_$?

Answer and Explanation: d. $a + b$ is $5 + 7 = 12$. $c \times d$ is $3 \times 2 = 6$. $12 \div 6 = 2$. As a letter, this is d. Make sure to give your answer as a letter! It is an extremely common mistake that students write down the number they have calculated instead of the letter, contrary to what is asked for. In this question, it is important to follow BODMAS / BIDMAS. First, do the sums inside the brackets, then do the division between the two sums afterwards. Here, it is especially important not to neglect the brackets, as without the brackets $a + b$ would be lower down in the priority when doing the calculation, which would result in a different answer.

Tips: Many students, despite it being underlined, forget to put their answers in letters. There will be a few questions in whatever exam you sit that really test your ability to read the information carefully. Do not lose focus. Secondly, make sure to follow BODMAS / BIDMAS on a question like this, and do not worry that you are mixing numbers and letters - letters behave exactly as numbers do. Keep in mind that certain abbreviations exist, however. For example, you may see $c \times d$ written as cd. This is the sort of question where there are lots of little tricks to be aware of.

Now Try This Question: Using the provided code, complete the following sums writing your answer in **letters**:

$a = 5, b = 7, c = 3, d = 2, e = 8$

What is: $b \times d - c - e = \_\_$?

Answer: c

Question Type-Ordered Walkthrough

20) **HIDDEN WORDS**

Sample Question: A four letter word is hidden between two words in the sentence below. These two words are always next to each other, but there may be punctuation between them. Find this four letter word from one of the options. Write your chosen option below:
Example:

Q. Tom kicked the ball over the fence.
A. Love = ball over

Question:

It was slightly painful to get two extra injections before I travel on holiday.

A. before I

B. extra injections

C. painful to

D. get an

E. two extra

Answer and Explanation: B, extra injections. These questions test your vocabulary of words, and to think outside of the box and spot hidden words. Look at your sentence, and look between each word. "It was" are the first two words. Join them together and see if you can find a word. Itwas. Twas could be considered an old English word, however it would be written as 'twas and is therefore not acceptable. The next two words are 'was slightly'. There are no words when you join these together. As you move through each word systematically, you reach 'extra injection'. Extrainjection. Here you can see a word, 'rain', formed between the two. This is the answer, B.

Tips: Go through each part of the sentence two words at a time, and look at the combination of 3 letters from the first word and 1 from the second word. Next, 2 letters from each, and then 1 letter from the first word and 3 letters from the second word. This way you cannot miss the answer, as long as you are not careless of course! You will get faster and faster at this screening process with practice.

Now Try This Question: A four letter word is hidden between two words in the sentence below. These two words are always next to each other, but there may be punctuation between them. Find this four letter word from one of the options. Write your chosen option below.

Question:

A trip to a spa involves having a meal with friends as well.

A. trip to

B. having a

C. friends as

D. meal with

E. spa involves

Answer: E

Verbal Reasoning - Test 16

Time allowed for this paper : 60 minutes

Instructions for Best Practice:

> Attempt all of the questions.
> Ensure that your answers are clearly marked in the answer boxes.
> Calculators and rulers must not be used.
> Equipment recommended: 2 x Pencil & 1 x Eraser.

Verbal Reasoning - Test 16

1) Three consecutive letters have been taken out of a word. Select which three letters have been omitted from the options. Write your answer below:

   The dinosaur SKE___ON was found buried underground.

   A. LIP
   B. LIT
   C. LAP
   D. LET
   E. LOW

   Answer:

2) You are required to move one letter from the first word to the second word, creating two new words. Write your answer below:

   STREAM STOKE

   Answer:

3) Write the letter that will complete the word in front of the brackets and begin the word after the brackets. The SAME letter must fit into BOTH sets of brackets. Write your answer below:

   sho (_) ase, har (_) ast

   Answer:

4) Select the two words inside the brackets that are connected in some way to the words outside the brackets. Write your answer below:

   Caroline only like certain types of animals. She likes the SNAKE LIZARD (goldfish, frog, antelope, turtle, iguana)

   Answer:

5) Find the pair of letters that will complete the sentence in the best way. The alphabet is provided below to help you. Write your answer below:

   A B C D E F G H I J K L M N O P Q R S T U V W X Y Z

   IC is to FE as WO is to ___?

   Answer:

6) Select the pair of words, one from each group that are most opposite in meaning to each other from the options given below. Write your answer below:

   The opposite of (expose, shut, door) is (window, hide, lay).

   A. Expose hide
   B. Expose lay
   C. Shut hide
   D. Door window
   E. Expose window

   Answer:

7) Choose the correct answer for the following problem. Write your answer below:

   £1 is equivalent to 4.5 Peruvian soles. How much is £6.50 worth is Peruvian soles?

   A. 26.50 soles
   B. 27.25 soles
   C. 28.50 soles
   D. 29.25 soles
   E. 30.50 soles

   Answer:

8) Read the information provided and choose the single best answer for the question. Write your answer below:

   Four children, Sid, Kate, Jay and Priya all had a birthday today.
   In one years time, Priya will be the age Sid is now.
   Jay is half of Kate's age and is three years younger than Priya.
   Priya is 11 years old.

   What age is Kate now?

   A. 6   D. 14
   B. 8   E. 16
   C. 12

   Answer:

9) Read the information provided and choose the single best answer for the question. Write your answer below:

   Four children, Sid, Kate, Jay and Priya all had a birthday today.
   In one years time, Priya will be the age Sid is now.
   Jay is half of Kate's age and is three years younger than Priya.
   Priya is 11 years old.

   What age will Jay be when Priya is 15 years old?

   A. 6   D. 14
   B. 8   E. 16
   C. 12

   Answer:

10) The words in brackets are formed from the main word. Identify the pattern to work out the missing word from the options given. Write your answer below:

    Bones (son), caper (rap), delve (?)

    A. EEL
    B. DEE
    C. VEE
    D. VEL
    E. ELD

    Answer:

Verbal Reasoning - Test 16

11) A **four letter word** is hidden between two words in the sentence below. These **two words** are always next to each other, but there **may be punctuation between** them. Find this **four letter word** from one of the options. Write your answer below:

It's not every day you come across a famous footballer!

A. come across
B. a famous
C. day you
D. famous footballer
E. not every

Answer:

12) A **four letter word** is hidden between two words in the sentence below. These **two words** are always next to each other, but there **may be punctuation between** them. Find this **four letter word** from one of the options. Write your answer below:

The flamenco always has a special place in my heart.

A. flamenco always
B. special place
C. my heart
D. a special
E. always has

Answer:

13) Find the number that best complete the series. Fill in the missing blank with one of the following options and write your answer below:

2, 4, 8, 16, 32, ___

A. 46
B. 52
C. 32
D. 64
E. 48

Answer:

14) Find one word **from each group** that together makes **one correctly spelt word**. The letters **must not be rearranged**. The word from the first group **must always be used first**. Write your answer below:

They found a handy (pocket, hole, place) (pamphlet, book, time) in her purse.

A. Holebook   D. Placepamphlet
B. Pocketbook   E. Placetime
C. Pockettime

Answer:

15) Find the pair of letters that will continue the series. The alphabet is provided below to help you. Write your answer below:

A B C D E F G H I J K L M N O P Q R S T U V W X Y Z

CD, BC, AB, ZA, YZ, ___ ?

Answer:

16) Select the pair of words, one from each group that are most **opposite in meaning** to each other from the options given. Write your answer below:

The opposite of (flexible, hard, power) is (tough, soft, squeeze).

A. Flexible soft
B. Hard soft
C. Power squeeze
D. Hard tough
E. Power tough

Answer:

17) Select the **TWO odd words** from the options given. Write your answer below:

Money, dollars, euros, Europe, sterling

A. Money dollars
B. Dollars sterling
C. Sterling Europe
D. Money Europe
E. Europe euros

Answer:

18) Choose the correct answer by **completing the following functions and sums** with the **correct numbers and signs** as appropriate. Write your answer below:

6 ÷ ___ + 2 − 5 = 0

A. 0
B. 1
C. 2
D. 3
E. 4

Answer:

19) Choose the correct answer for the following problem. Write your answer below:

Three times a number plus seven is 70. What is twice that number minus 7?

A. 33
B. 35
C. 37
D. 39
E. 41

Answer:

20) Three consecutive letters are removed from the word in CAPITALS. These letters make a word. From the options, find the missing letters to complete the sentence. Write your answer below:

The police were able to TR the call.

A. ACE
B. AND
C. EAT
D. ONE
E. EAR

Answer:

Verbal Reasoning - Test 16

21) In each set of numbers, the number in the brackets is related to the two numbers either side of it. Find this relation to work out the missing number '(?)' in the third set. Choose one of the options and write your answer below:

18 (6) 12, 9 (3) 6, 7 (?) 4

A. 13
B. 3
C. 24
D. 7
E. 11

Answer:

22) In each set of numbers, the number in the brackets is related to the two numbers either side of it. Find this relation to work out the missing number '(?)' in the third set. Choose one of the option and write your answer below:

41 (14) 27, 18 (2) 16, 12 (?) 12

A. 4
B. 19
C. 13
D. 2
E. 0

Answer:

23) Select the word from the brackets that will complete the sentence in the most sensible way. Write your answer below:

Suit is to DRESS as trousers is to (skirt, shoes, ring)

Answer:

24) Find one word from each group that together makes one correctly spelt word. The letters must not be rearranged. The word from the first group must always be used first. Write your answer below:

They filled the (flower, tree, rose) (place, pot, vase) with a beautiful bush.

A. Flowervase
B. Treepot
C. Roseplace
D. Flowerpot
E. Treeplace

Answer:

25) Find the pair of letters that will continue the series. The alphabet is provided below to help you. Write your answer below:

A B C D E F G H I J K L M N O P Q R S T U V W X Y Z

HI, GK, FM, EO, DQ, __?

Answer:

26) Using the provided code, complete the following sums writing your answer in numbers:

a = 3, b = 12, c = 0, d = 5, e = 8

Solve: b ÷ a + d = __?

Answer:

27) Using the provided code, complete the following sums writing your answer in numbers:

a = 3, b = 12, c = 0, d = 5, e = 8

Solve: d × c + e = __?

Answer:

28) Write the letter that will complete the word in front of the brackets and begin the word after the brackets. The SAME letter must fit into BOTH sets of brackets. Write your answer below:

bal (_) imp, hal (_) ast

Answer:

29) Select the two words inside the brackets that are connected in some way to the words outside the brackets. Write your answer below:

SHARK WHALE (goldfish, catfish, frog, turtle, monkey)

Answer:

30) Select the word from the brackets that will complete the sentence in the most sensible way. Write your answer below:

Television is to WATCH as book is to (see, read, buy)

Answer:

Verbal Reasoning - Test 16

31) Find the pair of letters that will complete the sentence in the best way. The alphabet is provided below to help you. Write your answer below:

A B C D E F G H I J K L M N O P Q R S T U V W X Y Z

SU is to RV as IK is to ___?

Answer:

32) Select the TWO odd words from the options given. Write your answer below:

Kilograms, pounds, weight, mass, tonnes

A. Kilograms mass
B. Weight mass
C. Tonnes pounds
D. Pounds kilograms
E. Pounds weight

Answer:

33) Choose the correct answer by completing the following functions and sums with the correct numbers and signs as appropriate. Write your answer below:

168 + 12 − ___ = 165 + 7

A. 8
B. 10
C. 12
D. 14
E. 16

Answer:

34) The words in brackets are formed from the main word. Identify the pattern to work out the missing word from the options given. Write your answer below:

Erase (era), gates (sat), gangster (?)

A. GET
B. SANG
C. SAT
D. SET
E. RAN

Answer:

35) Find the number that best complete the series. Fill in the missing blank with one of the following options and write your answer below:

1, 1, 2, 6, 24, ___

A. 38
B. 120
C. 100
D. 96
E. 59

Answer:

36) Three consecutive letters have been taken out of a word. Select which three letters have been omitted from the options. Write your answer below:

The SH____ swam towards the helpless penguin.

A. ASK
B. ARM
C. ACT
D. ANT
E. ARK

Answer:

37) You are required to move one letter from the first word to the second word, creating two new words. Write your answer below:

CAPE HARM

The _____ had a remarkable _____ about him in the zoo.

Answer:

38) Work out the relationship between the word and the code to solve the code and write your answer below:

A B C D E F G H I J K L M N O P Q R S T U V W X Y Z

CIRCLE is to BGOYGY. What is the code for OVAL?

Answer:

39) Work out the relationship between the word and the code to solve the code and write your answer below:

A B C D E F G H I J K L M N O P Q R S T U V W X Y Z

CIRCLE is to BGOYGY. What is the code for SQUARE?

Answer:

40) Three consecutive letters are removed from the word in CAPITALS. These letters make a word. From the options, find the missing letters to complete the sentence. Write your answer below:

Paula went to the theatre to watch the PERFORCE.

A. CAN
B. BAN
C. MAN
D. MAP
E. CAP

Answer:

Verbal Reasoning

Verbal Reasoning - Test 17

Time allowed for this paper : 60 minutes

Instructions for Best Practice:

> Attempt all of the questions.
> Ensure that your answers are clearly marked in the answer boxes.
> Calculators and rulers must not be used.
> Equipment recommended: 2 x Pencil & 1 x Eraser.

Verbal Reasoning - Test 17

Marks

1) Three consecutive letters have been taken out of a word. Select which three letters have been omitted from the options. Write your answer below:

   He sat on his computer, ready to D____LOAD the file.

   A. OAT
   B. OUT
   C. OWN
   D. BAT
   E. BUT

   Answer:

2) You are required to move one letter from the first word to the second word, creating two new words. Write your answer below:

   BONE READ.

   Answer:

3) Write the letter that will complete the word in front of the brackets and begin the word after the brackets. The SAME letter must fit into BOTH sets of brackets. Write your answer below:

   gam (_) ars, tre (_) ach

   Answer:

4) Select the two words inside the brackets that are connected in some way to the words outside the brackets. Write your answer below:

   TENNIS ROUNDERS (jogging, squash, cricket, javelin, swimming)

   Answer:

5) Select the pair of words, one from each group that are most opposite in meaning to each other from the options given below. Write your answer below:

   The opposite of (fry, bake, boil) is (cool, fridge, freeze).

   A. Fry cool
   B. Bake freeze
   C. Boil freeze
   D. Bake fridge
   E. Boil cool

   Answer:

6) Select the TWO odd words from the options given. Write your answer below:

   Mansion, garden, cottage, park, bungalow

   A. Garden park
   B. Cottage mansion
   C. Park bungalow
   D. Mansion garden
   E. Bungalow cottage

   Answer:

7) Choose the correct answer by completing the following functions and sums with the correct numbers and signs as appropriate. Write your answer below:

   528 = 16 × 32 + ___

   A. 13
   B. 14
   C. 16
   D. 18
   E. 19

   Answer:

8) The words in brackets are formed from the main word. Identify the pattern to work out the missing word from the options given. Write your answer below:

   Metal (let), opera (ape), lines (?)

   A. LIS
   B. NIL
   C. SIN
   D. ELN
   E. LES

   Answer:

9) Three consecutive letters are removed from the word in CAPITALS. These letters make a word. From the options, find the missing letters to complete the sentence. Write your answer below:

   Charlotte stood in the SE as it was a hot day.

   A. HID
   B. HAT
   C. HAD
   D. HOP
   E. HIP

   Answer:

10) Three consecutive letters are removed from the word in CAPITALS. These letters make a word. From the options, find the missing letters to complete the sentence. Write your answer below:

    Vijay put the milk in the FGE.

    A. RAP
    B. RID
    C. RAT
    D. RUN
    E. RIP

    Answer:

Verbal Reasoning - Test 17

11) In each set of numbers, the number in the brackets is related to **the two numbers either side of it**. Find this relation to work out the missing number '(?)' in the third set. Choose one of the options and write your answer below:

15 (2) 13, 17 (6) 11, 8 (?) 3

A. 5
B. 11
C. 20
D. 21
E. 18

Answer:

12) In each set of numbers, the number in the brackets is related to **the two numbers either side of it**. Find this relation to work out the missing number '(?)' in the third set. Choose one of the option and write your answer below:

19 (2) 17, 5 (1) 4, 7 (?) 2

A. 12
B. 5
C. 9
D. 23
E. 20

Answer:

13) Find the number that best complete the series. Fill in the missing blank with one of the following options and write your answer below:

2, 6, 18, 54, ___

A. 120
B. 162
C. 178
D. 144
E. 158

Answer:

14) Find the pair of letters that will continue the series. The alphabet is provided below to help you. Write your answer below:

A B C D E F G H I J K L M N O P Q R S T U V W X Y Z

BO, ER, HU, KX, NA, ___?

Answer:

15) Find the pair of letters that will complete the sentence in the best way. The alphabet is provided below to help you. Write your answer below:

A B C D E F G H I J K L M N O P Q R S T U V W X Y Z

FU is to IS as HR is to ___

Answer:

16) Using the provided code, complete the following sums writing your answer in numbers:

a = 3, b = 12, c = 0, d = 5, e = 8

Solve: a + d − e × c = ___?

Answer:

17) Using the provided code, complete the following sums writing your answer in numbers:

a = 3, b = 12, c = 0, d = 5, e = 8

Solve: b − a + d = ___?

Answer:

18) Write the letter that will complete the word in front of the brackets and begin the word after the brackets. The SAME letter must fit into BOTH sets of brackets. Write your answer below:

hai (_) are, pea (_) est

Answer:

19) Select the two words inside the brackets that are connected in some way to the words outside the brackets. Write your answer below:

James found the following in his kitchen. An OVEN, MICROWAVE (bed, dishwasher, sofa, bath, toaster)

Answer:

20) Three consecutive letters have been taken out of a word. Select which three letters have been omitted from the options. Write your answer below:

The dog ate the SC____S left on the floor near the bin.

A. RIT
B. RAP
C. TAP
D. BIT
E. RAT

Answer:

Verbal Reasoning - Test 17

21) You are required to move one letter from the first word to the second word, creating **two new words**. Write your answer below:

BROW PAT

Answer:

22) Work out the relationship between the word and the code to solve the code and write your answer below:

A B C D E F G H I J K L M N O P Q R S T U V W X Y Z

CIRCLE is to BGOYGY. What is the code for RECTANGLE?

Answer:

23) Work out the relationship between the word and the code to solve the code and write your answer below:

A B C D E F G H I J K L M N O P Q R S T U V W X Y Z

CIRCLE is to BGOYGY.

<u>Decode</u> the following: SPFWIAEW?

Answer:

24) Find one word from each group that together makes **one correctly spelt word**. The letters **must not be rearranged**. The word from the first group **must always be used first**. Write your answer below:

He placed a (head, neck, ear) (lace, tie, cord) on his wife's neck.

A. Headtie
B. Necklace
C. Earcord
D. Headcord
E. Earlace

Answer:

25) Find the pair of letters that will continue the series. The alphabet is provided below to help you. Write your answer below:

A B C D E F G H I J K L M N O P Q R S T U V W X Y Z

ST, RQ, QN, PK, OH, ___?

Answer:

26) Find the pair of letters that will complete the sentence in the best way. The alphabet is provided below to help you. Write your answer below:

A B C D E F G H I J K L M N O P Q R S T U V W X Y Z

UB is to WD as ZH is to ___

Answer:

27) Select the pair of words, one from each group that are **most opposite in meaning** to each other from the options given. Write your answer below:

The opposite of (draw, cancel, paper) is (erase, pencil, mark).

A. Draw erase
B. Cancel mark
C. Paper mark
D. Draw pencil
E. Cancel erase

Answer:

28) Select the TWO odd words from the options given. Write your answer below:

Hours, watch, minute, clock, seconds

A. Minute seconds
B. Hours clock
C. Minute watch
D. Hours seconds
E. Watch clock

Answer:

29) Choose the correct answer by completing the following functions and sums with the correct numbers and signs as appropriate. Write your answer below:

(8 + ___) ÷ 4 = (6 × 4) ÷ 3

A. 20
B. 24
C. 28
D. 32
E. 36

Answer:

30) Read the information provided and choose the single best answer for the question. Write your answer below:

Four children, Sid, Kate, Jay and Priya all had a birthday today.
In one years time, Priya will be the age Sid is now.
Jay is half of Kate's age and is three years younger than Priya.
Priya is 11 years old.

What age is Jay now?

A. 6   D. 14
B. 8   E. 16
C. 12

Answer:

Verbal Reasoning - Test 17

31) A four letter word is hidden between two words in the sentence below. These two words are always next to each other, but there may be punctuation between them. Find this four letter word from one of the options. Write your answer below:

Do you know about the origin of Tabasco? All you need to know is in this book!

A. you know
B. this book
C. know is
D. origin of
E. Tabasco all

Answer:

32) A four letter word is hidden between two words in the sentence below. These two words are always next to each other, but there may be punctuation between them. Find this four letter word from one of the options. Write your answer below:

In her house, her portico always allows plenty of light in.

A. house her
B. allows plenty
C. portico always
D. of light
E. her house

Answer:

33) Find the number that best complete the series. Fill in the missing blank with one of the following options and write your answer below:

2, 4, 12, 48, ___

A. 96
B. 110
C. 230
D. 182
E. 240

Answer:

34) Select the word from the brackets that will complete the sentence in the most sensible way. Write your answer below:

Bed is to BEDROOM as oven is to (bathroom, lounge, kitchen)

Answer:

35) Find one word from each group that together makes one correctly spelt word. The letters must not be rearranged. The word from the first group must always be used first. Write your answer below:

The boy made a (needle, stick, pin) (area, gap, hole) camera in his science class.

A. Needlearea
B. Pinhole
C. Needlegap
D. Stickhole
E. Pingap

Answer:

36) Choose the correct answer for the following problem. Write your answer below:

Throughout the winter, a horse eats one-third of its bales of hay and ignores 44 bales of hay. How many bales of hay did the horse eat?

A. 18
B. 19
C. 20
D. 21
E. 22

Answer:

37) Choose the correct answer for the following problem. Write your answer below:
A television programme began at 16.55 and lasted for 55 minutes. Shiv missed the first 15 minutes but saw the rest of the programme. How long did Shiv watch for?

A. 30 mins
B. 35 mins
C. 40 mins
D. 45 mins
E. 50 mins

Answer:

38) Read the information provided and choose the single best answer for the question. Write your answer below:

Jess is now three times as old as Tim will be in 5 years' time. In 5 years Jess will be 29 years old.

What age is Jess now?

A. 21   D. 24
B. 22   E. 25
C. 23

Answer:

39) The words in brackets are formed from the main word. Identify the pattern to work out the missing word from the options given. Write your answer below:

Learnt (tea), layer (ray), lower (?)

A. ROW
B. WEL
C. ROL
D. LER
E. LOW

Answer:

40) Select the word from the brackets that will complete the sentence in the most sensible way. Write your answer below:

Monkey is to MAMMAL as lizard is to (fish, reptile, insect)

Answer:

Verbal Reasoning - Test 18

Time allowed for this paper : 60 minutes

Instructions for Best Practice:

> Attempt all of the questions.
> Ensure that your answers are clearly marked in the answer boxes.
> Calculators and rulers must not be used.
> Equipment recommended: 2 x Pencil & 1 x Eraser.

Verbal Reasoning - Test 18

1) Using the provided code, complete the following sums writing your answer in numbers:

   apple = 11, bike = 1, car = 4, desk = 5, egg = 6

   Solve: apple − desk + bike = ___?

   Answer:

2) Write the letter that will complete the word in front of the brackets and begin the word after the brackets. The SAME letter must fit into BOTH sets of brackets. Write your answer below:

   har (_) ast, dam (_) eak

   Answer:

3) Find the pair of letters that will complete the sentence in the best way. The alphabet is provided below to help you. Write your answer below:

   A B C D E F G H I J K L M N O P Q R S T U V W X Y Z

   RS is to QT as EF is to ___?

   Answer:

4) Select the pair of words, one from each group that are most opposite in meaning to each other from the options given below. Write your answer below:

   The opposite of (clean, wash, water) is (mud, clear, dirty).

   A. Wash mud
   B. Water dirty
   C. Water mud
   D. Clean dirty
   E. Water clear

   Answer:

5) Read the information provided and choose the single best answer for the question. Write your answer below:

   Jess is now three times as old as Tim will be in 5 years' time. In 5 years Jess will be 29 years old.

   What age is Tim now?

   A. 1   D. 4
   B. 2   E. 5
   C. 3

   Answer:

6) Read the information provided and choose the single best answer for the question. Write your answer below:

   Jess is now three times as old as Tim will be in 5 years' time. In 5 years Jess will be 29 years old.
   What age will Tim be in 8 years?

   A. 11
   B. 12
   C. 13
   D. 14
   E. 15

   Answer:

7) The words in brackets are formed from the main word. Identify the pattern to work out the missing word from the options given. Write your answer below:

   Layer (ray), large (ear), latch (?)

   A. LAT
   B. CAT
   C. HAT
   D. LAH
   E. EAR

   Answer:

8) In each set of numbers, the number in the brackets is related to the two numbers either side of it. Find this relation to work out the missing number '(?)' in the third set. Choose one of the options and write your answer below:

   3 (1) 2, 9 (2) 7, 16 (?) 8

   A. 21
   B. 11
   C. 8
   D. 1
   E. 15

   Answer:

9) In each set of numbers, the number in the brackets is related to the two numbers either side of it. Find this relation to work out the missing number '(?)' in the third set. Choose one of the option and write your answer below:

   14 (2) 12, 17 (6) 11, 15 (?) 4

   A. 15
   B. 17
   C. 8
   D. 20
   E. 11

   Answer:

10) A four letter word is hidden between two words in the sentence below. These two words are always next to each other, but there may be punctuation between them. Find this four letter word from one of the options. Write your answer below:

    She always allows strangers near her children, which is really dangerous.

    A. near her
    B. children which
    C. is really
    D. strangers near
    E. she always

    Answer:

Verbal Reasoning

Verbal Reasoning - Test 18

11) A **four letter word** is hidden between two words in the sentence below. These **two words are always next to each other**, but there **may be punctuation between** them. Find this **four letter word** from one of the options. Write your answer below:

You must all be careful who you share this important information with.

- A. be careful
- B. must all
- C. You must
- D. you share
- E. information with

Answer:

12) Find the number that **best complete the series**. Fill in the **missing blank** with one of the following options and write your answer below:

1 apple, 3 apples, 9 apples, 27 apples, ___ apples?

- A. 36
- B. 45
- C. 81
- D. 62
- E. 73

Answer:

13) Find the number that **best complete the series**. Fill in the **missing blank** with one of the following options and write your answer below:

2, 6, 4, 12, 8, 24, ___?

- A. 16
- B. 12
- C. 20
- D. 10
- E. 14

Answer:

14) **Three consecutive letters** have been taken out of a word. Select which three letters **have been omitted** from the options. Write your answer below:

The king made a grand ENT___CE.

- A. RUN
- B. RAT
- C. RAN
- D. CAN
- E. CUT

Answer:

15) You are required to move one letter from the first word to the second word, creating **two new words**. Write your answer below:

HUNT SIP

Answer:

16) Select the two words **inside the brackets** that are connected in some way to the words **outside the brackets**. Write your answer below:

BLUE ORANGE (sky, yellow, pear, banana, green)

Answer:

17) Select the word from the brackets that will **complete the sentence in the most sensible way**. Write your answer below:

Cow is to CALF as goat is to (baby, kid, lamb)

Answer:

18) Find the **pair of letters** that will complete the sentence in the best way. The alphabet is provided below to help you. Write your answer below:

A B C D E F G H I J K L M N O P Q R S T U V W X Y Z

KM is to IN as AD is to ___?

Answer:

19) Select the pair of words, one from each group that are **most opposite in meaning** to each other from the options given. Write your answer below:

The opposite of (Good Thing Today) is (Look Bad Now).

- A. Thing Back
- B. Good Bad
- C. Today Now
- D. Look Today
- E. Good Now

Answer:

20) Select the **TWO odd words** from the options given. Write your answer below:

Wood, chair, box, plastic, steel, silk, iron

- A. Chair steel
- B. Box plastic
- C. Chair box
- D. Chair wood
- E. Wood steel

Answer:

Verbal Reasoning - Test 18

Marks

21) Choose the correct answer for the following problem. Write your answer below:

Aaran has 45p. If Xi had 12p more, she would have the same as Puja. If Aaran spent one-third of his money, he would also have the same as Puja. How much does Xi have?

A. 14p
B. 16p
C. 18p
D. 20p
E. 22p

Answer:

22) The words in brackets are formed from the main word. Identify the pattern to work out the missing word from the options given. Write your answer below:

Tiger (rig), hints (sin), seats (?)

A. SAT
B. SEA
C. ATE
D. TEA
E. TAS

Answer:

23) Three consecutive letters are removed from the word in CAPITALS. These letters make a word. From the options, find the missing letters to complete the sentence. Write your answer below:

Bob walked in through the ENTCE.

A. CAN
B. CUT
C. RUN
D. RAN
E. RAT

Answer:

24) Three consecutive letters have been taken out of a word. Select which three letters have been omitted from the options. Write your answer below:

Hasan was asked by his mother to CH___ the milk to butter.

A. URN
B. END
C. HAT
D. SIP
E. ARK

Answer:

25) You are required to move one letter from the first word to the second word, creating two new words. Write your answer below:

SCAN END

Answer:

26) Work out the relationship between the word and the code to solve the code and write your answer below:

A B C D E F G H I J K L M N O P Q R S T U V W X Y Z

CIRCLE is to BGOYGY. Decode the following: GCUWBIG

Answer:

27) Work out the relationship between the word and the code to solve the code and write your answer below:

A B C D E F G H I J K L M N O P Q R S T U V W X Y Z

CIRCLE is to BGOYGY. Decode the following: BSYA.

Answer:

28) Using the provided code, complete the following sums writing your answer in numbers:

a = 3, b = 12, c = 0, d = 5, e = 8

Solve: e + d × c + a = ___?

Answer:

29) Write the letter that will complete the word in front of the brackets and begin the word after the brackets. The SAME letter must fit into BOTH sets of brackets. Write your answer below:

cra (_) oat, dra (_) eat

Answer:

30) Select the two words inside the brackets that are connected in some way to the words outside the brackets. Write your answer below:

James had a number of items in his bedroom. He had a BED, CUPBOARD (table, fridge, house, chair, sleep)

Answer:

Verbal Reasoning - Test 18

31) Select the word from the brackets that will complete the sentence in the most sensible way. Write your answer below:

Sheep is to LAMB as horse is to (foal, kid, child)

Answer:

32) Find one word from each group that together makes one correctly spelt word. The letters must not be rearranged. The word from the first group must always be used first. Write your answer below:

The toddler made sure he brushed his teeth using a (mouth, tooth, tongue) (brush, comb, band).

A. Mouthbrush   D. Mouthband
B. Tongueband   E. Mouthcomb
C. Toothbrush

Answer:

33) Find one word from each group that together makes one correctly spelt word. The letters must not be rearranged. The word from the first group must always be used first. Write your answer below:

The bees attempted to protect their precious (honey, sugar, nectar) (brush, comb, band).

A. Honeybrush   D. Honeycomb
B. Sugarband   E. Sugarbrush
C. Nectarcomb

Answer:

34) Find the pair of letters that will continue the series. The alphabet is provided below to help you. Write your answer below:

A B C D E F G H I J K L M N O P Q R S T U V W X Y Z

BM, DP, FS, HV, JY __?

Answer:

35) Find the pair of letters that will continue the series. The alphabet is provided below to help you. Write your answer below:

A B C D E F G H I J K L M N O P Q R S T U V W X Y Z

MP, NO, ON, PM, QL, __?

Answer:

36) Select the TWO odd words from the options given. Write your answer below:

Run, sleep, bed, walk, chair

A. Run walk
B. Bed chair
C. Run sleep
D. Chair walk
E. Chair sleep

Answer:

37) Choose the correct answer by completing the following functions and sums with the correct numbers and signs as appropriate. Write your answer below:

58 + (__ × 3) = 7 × 10 − 6

A. 9
B. 6
C. 4
D. 3
E. 2

Answer:

38) Three consecutive letters are removed from the word in CAPITALS. These letters make a word. From the options, find the missing letters to complete the sentence. Write your answer below:

Natasha used SPOO to wash her hair.

A. HIM
B. HUT
C. HAM
D. BUT
E. PUT

Answer:

39) Choose the correct answer by completing the following functions and sums with the correct numbers and signs as appropriate. Write your answer below:

73 − 26 × 2 = __ × 5 − 4

A. 4
B. 5
C. 7
D. 9
E. 12

Answer:

40) Choose the correct answer for the following problem. Write your answer below:

In a garden there are three types of flowers. One third of them are daffodils, a quarter of the rest are roses. There are 30 tulips in the garden. How many roses are there?

A. 8
B. 10
C. 12
D. 14
E. 16

Answer:

Verbal Reasoning - Test 19

Time allowed for this paper : 60 minutes

Instructions for Best Practice:

> Attempt all of the questions.
> Ensure that your answers are clearly marked in the answer boxes.
> Calculators and rulers must not be used.
> Equipment recommended: 2 x Pencil & 1 x Eraser.

Verbal Reasoning - Test 19

1) Choose the correct answer by **completing the following functions and sums** with the **correct numbers and signs** as appropriate. Write your answer below:

54 ÷ 6 + 3 = ___ ÷ 3

A. 27
B. 30
C. 33
D. 36
E. 39

Answer:

2) Choose the correct answer **for the following problem**. Write your answer below:

When three is subtracted from seven times a number, the answer is 60. What is the number?

A. 6
B. 7
C. 8
D. 9
E. 10

Answer:

3) The words in brackets are formed from the main word. **Identify the pattern** to work out the **missing word** from the options given. Write your answer below:

Bones (son), total (lot), feast (?)

A. FET
B. SAT
C. TEA
D. EAT
E. ATE

Answer:

4) Three consecutive letters are removed from the word in CAPITALS. These letters make a word. From the options, find the missing letters to complete the sentence. Write your answer below:

The teacher was ASED of the behaviour of her class.

A. ARK
B. ART
C. ARM
D. HAT
E. HAM

Answer:

5) A **four letter word** is hidden between two words in the sentences below. These **two words are always next to each** other, but there **may be punctuation between** them. Find this **four letter word** from one of the options. Write your answer below:

This taco really brings a tear to my eye! It is so tasty!

A. a tear
B. my eye
C. taco really
D. brings a
E. so tasty

Answer:

6) A **four letter word** is hidden between two words in the sentence below. These **two words are always next to each** other, but there **may be punctuation between** them. Find this **four letter word** from one of the options. Write your answer below:

I play for my local football team as a defender, but I want to be the next big star and play up front.

A. next big
B. and play
C. local football
D. football team
E. team as

Answer:

7) Select the two words **inside the brackets** that are connected in some way to the words **outside the brackets**. Write your answer below:

DEER COW (rabbit, lion, cheetah, tiger, mouse)

Answer:

8) Select the word from the brackets that will **complete the sentence in the most sensible way**. Write your answer below:

Seed is to TREE as egg is to (plant, food, hen)

Answer:

9) Work **out the relationship** between the word and the code to solve the code and write your answer below:

A B C D E F G H I J K L M N O P Q R S T U V W X Y Z

BOT is to APS. What is the code for CAR?

Answer:

10) Work **out the relationship** between the word and the code to solve the code and write your answer below:

A B C D E F G H I J K L M N O P Q R S T U V W X Y Z

BOT is to APS. What is the code for MOBILE?

Answer:

Verbal Reasoning - Test 19

11) Using the provided code, complete the following sums writing your answer in numbers:

aaa = 11, bbb = 1, ccc = 4, ddd = 5, eee = 6

Solve: ddd × ccc − aaa = ___?

Answer:

12) Using the provided code, complete the following sums writing your answer in numbers:

aaa = 11, bbb = 1, ccc = 4, ddd = 5, eee = 6

Solve: ccc + ddd + eee = ___?

Answer:

13) Write the letter that will **complete the word in front of the brackets** and **begin the word after the brackets**. The SAME letter must fit into BOTH sets of brackets. Write your answer below:

nea (_) ick, pos (_) rap

Answer:

14) Select the word from the brackets that will **complete the sentence in the most sensible way**. Write your answer below:

French is to FRANCE as Spanish is to (Spain, Italy, Germany)

Answer:

15) Find one word **from each group** that together makes **one correctly spelt word**. The letters **must not be rearranged**. The word from the first group **must always** be used first. Write your answer below:

The young adventurer ventured through the (sleet, snow, rain) (wood, tree, forest).

A. Rainforest   D. Rainwood
B. Snowtree   E. Snowforest
C. Sleetwood

Answer:

16) Select the TWO odd words from the options given. Write your answer below:

Bread, milk, cow, butter, yoghurt

A. Milk butter
B. Butter bread
C. Yoghurt cow
D. Cow milk
E. Bread cow

Answer:

17) Choose the correct answer by **completing the following functions and sums** with the **correct numbers and signs** as appropriate. Write your answer below:

243 + 65 = 14 × 18 + ___

A. 64
B. 53
C. 56
D. 58
E. 69

Answer:

18) Three consecutive letters are removed from the word in CAPITALS. These letters make a word. From the options, find the missing letters to complete the sentence. Write your answer below:

Ali glared in FRUSTION at Jamie's bad joke.

A. RAM
B. RAP
C. RAT
D. ROT
E. RAN

Answer:

19) In each set of numbers, the number in the brackets is related to **the two numbers either side of it**. Find this relation to work out the missing number '(?)' in the third set. Choose one of the options and write your answer below:

29 (14) 15, 31 (12) 19, 17 (?) 15

A. 2
B. 8
C. 23
D. 3
E. 17

Answer:

20) In each set of numbers, the number in the brackets is related to **the two numbers either side of it**. Find this relation to work out the missing number '(?)' in the third set. Choose one of the option and write your answer below:

18 (5) 13, 27 (15) 12, 24 (?) 11

A. 19
B. 11
C. 13
D. 5
E. 1

Answer:

Verbal Reasoning - Test 19

21) Find the number that best complete the series. Fill in the missing blank with one of the following options and write your answer below:

3, 10, 12, 40, 48, 160, ___

A. 188
B. 168
C. 142
D. 192
E. 120

Answer:

22) Find the pair of letters that will complete the sentence in the best way. The alphabet is provided below to help you. Write your answer below:

A B C D E F G H I J K L M N O P Q R S T U V W X Y Z

DA is to CE as PM is to ___?

Answer:

23) Select the two words inside the brackets that are connected in some way to the words outside the brackets. Write your answer below:

GRAM POUND (metre, kilogram, dollar, ounce, euro)

Answer:

24) Find one word from each group that together makes one correctly spelt word. The letters must not be rearranged. The word from the first group must always be used first. Write your answer below:

Most of your work is done during the (day, night, morning) (week, hour, time).

A. Dayhour   D. Nighthour
B. Nighttime   E. Daytime
C. Morningweek

Answer:

25) Find the pair of letters that will continue the series. The alphabet is provided below to help you. Write your answer below:

A B C D E F G H I J K L M N O P Q R S T U V W X Y Z

11AT, 22YU, 33WV, 44UW, 22 ___?

Answer:

26) Select the pair of words, one from each group that are most opposite in meaning to each other from the options given. Write your answer below:

The opposite of (Fun Take Home) is (Beneath Boring Zoo).

A. Fun Beneath
B. Boring Home
C. Home Zoo
D. Fun Boring
E. Take Beneath

Answer:

27) Select the TWO odd words from the options given. Write your answer below:

mouse, monitor, keyboard, cat, paper

A. Cat paper
B. Mouse cat
C. Keyboard monitor
D. Monitor paper
E. Mouse keyboard

Answer:

28) Choose the correct answer for the following problem. Write your answer below:

Treble 12 is the same as four times a number. What is the number?

A. 4
B. 5
C. 7
D. 8
E. 9

Answer:

29) Read the information provided and choose the single best answer for the question. Write your answer below:

Will goes to the supermarket and at the self-checkout his total comes to £17.56
Will decides to pay using a £20 note and is given his change in the smallest possible number of coins. The coins dispensed by the self-checkout are 1p, 2p, 5p, 20p, 50p and £1.

How many £1 coins did he receive?

A. 0   D. 3
B. 1   E. 4
C. 2

Answer:

30) Read the information provided and choose the single best answer for the question. Write your answer below:

Will goes to the supermarket and at the self-checkout his total comes to £17.56
Will decides to pay using a £20 note and is given his change in the smallest possible number of coins. The coins dispensed by the self-checkout are 1p, 2p, 5p, 20p, 50p and £1.

How many 50p coins did he receive?

A. 0   D. 3
B. 1   E. 4
C. 2

Answer:

Verbal Reasoning - Test 19

31) The words in brackets are formed from the main word. Identify the pattern to work out the missing word from the options given. Write your answer below:

Aided (did), bathe (eat), beast (?)

A. BET
B. TEA
C. ATE
D. EAT
E. SAT

Answer:

36) Find the pair of letters that will continue the series. The alphabet is provided below to help you. Write your answer below:

A B C D E F G H I J K L M N O P Q R S T U V W X Y Z

NB, OD, PF, QH, RJ, ___?

Answer:

32) Find the number that best complete the series. Fill in the missing blank with one of the following options and write your answer below:

1, 5, 6, 11, 17, ___

A. 19
B. 21
C. 25
D. 28
E. 31

Answer:

37) Find the pair of letters that will complete the sentence in the best way. The alphabet is provided below to help you. Write your answer below:

A B C D E F G H I J K L M N O P Q R S T U V W X Y Z

GJ is DL as PR is to ___?

Answer:

33) Three consecutive letters have been taken out of a word. Select which three letters have been omitted from the options. Write your answer below:

The scenes at the brawl in South London were of absolute ___NAGE.

A. CAR
B. BAR
C. EAR
D. TAR
E. EAT

Answer:

38) Select the pair of words, one from each group that are most opposite in meaning to each other from the options given below. Write your answer below:

The opposite of (Sad Tree Bored) is (Make Happy Grass).

A. Sad Make
B. Happy Sad
C. Grass Life
D. Bored Make
E. Happy Tree

Answer:

34) You are required to move one letter from the first word to the second word, creating two new words. Write your answer below:

STRAY LOWLY

Answer:

39) Three consecutive letters have been taken out of a word. Select which three letters have been omitted from the options. Write your answer below:

They kept the food fresh inside the F___GE.

A. RIP
B. RAP
C. RUN
D. RID
E. RAT

Answer:

35) Write the letter that will complete the word in front of the brackets and begin the word after the brackets. The SAME letter must fit into BOTH sets of brackets. Write your answer below:

tos (_) ock, mis (_) alt

Answer:

40) You are required to move one letter from the first word to the second word, creating two new words. Write your answer below:

PLAICE SAD.

Answer:

Verbal Reasoning

Verbal Reasoning - Test 20

Time allowed for this paper : 60 minutes

Instructions for Best Practice:

> Attempt all of the questions.
> Ensure that your answers are clearly marked in the answer boxes.
> Calculators and rulers must not be used.
> Equipment recommended: 2 x Pencil & 1 x Eraser.

Verbal Reasoning - Test 20

1) Write the letter that will complete the word in front of the brackets and begin the word after the brackets. The SAME letter must fit into BOTH sets of brackets. Write your answer below:

   pin (_) ick, bel (_) ask

   Answer:

2) Select the two words **inside the brackets** that are connected in some way to the words **outside the brackets**. Write your answer below:

   CENTIPEDE BEETLE (dragonfly, bee, spider, wasp, ant)

   Answer:

3) **Find the pair of letters** that will continue the series. The alphabet is provided below to help you. Write your answer below:

   A B C D E F G H I J K L M N O P Q R S T U V W X Y Z

   BE, CG, DI, EK, FM, ___?

   Answer:

4) **Find the pair of letters** that will complete the sentence in the best way. The alphabet is provided below to help you. Write your answer below:

   A B C D E F G H I J K L M N O P Q R S T U V W X Y Z

   BM is to EJ as GT is to ___?

   Answer:

5) Choose the correct answer by **completing the following functions and sums with the correct numbers and signs** as appropriate. Write your answer below:

   (56 + 7) ÷ 7 = 3 × ___

   A. 3
   B. 4
   C. 5
   D. 6
   E. 7

   Answer:

6) Choose the correct answer for the following problem. Write your answer below:

   Subtracting five from a number is equivalent to nine multiplied by 8. What is the number?

   A. 68
   B. 63
   C. 79
   D. 74
   E. 77

   Answer:

7) **Read the information** provided and choose the single best answer for the question. Write your answer below:

   Will goes to the supermarket and at the self-checkout his total comes to £17.56.
   Will decides to pay using a £20 note and is given his change in the smallest possible number of coins. The coins dispensed by the self-checkout are 1p, 2p, 5p, 20p, 50p and £1.

   How many 2p coins did he receive?

   A. 0   D. 3
   B. 1   E. 4
   C. 2

   Answer:

8) **Three consecutive letters** have been taken out of a word. Select which three letters **have been omitted** from the options. Write your answer below:

   She had been on her PH____ for 30 minutes.

   A. ACE
   B. EAR
   C. ONE
   D. ALL
   E. EAT

   Answer:

9) You are required to move one letter from the first word to the second word, creating **two new words**. Write your answer below:

   CREASE STING

   Answer:

10) Select the word from the brackets that will **complete the sentence in the most sensible way**. Write your answer below:

    Laugh is to HAPPY as cry is to (envy, tears, sad)

    Answer:

Verbal Reasoning - Test 20

Marks

11) Find one word from each group that together makes one correctly spelt word. The letters must not be rearranged. The word from the first group must always be used first. Write your answer below:

James woke up and had a hearty (tear, rip, break) (quick, fast, slow).

A. Ripquick
B. Tearfast
C. Breakslow
D. Tearslow
E. Breakfast

Answer:

12) A four letter word is hidden between two words in the sentence below. These two words are always next to each other, but there may be punctuation between them. Find this four letter word from one of the options. Write your answer below:

What's the name of that tall striker who scored many goals for France?

A. tall striker
B. many goals
C. goals for
D. who scored
E. the name

Answer:

13) A four letter word is hidden between two words in the sentence below. These two words are always next to each other, but there may be punctuation between them. Find this four letter word from one of the options. Write your answer below:

This year, students who attended the school disco also got to see an international band perform.

A. see an
B. an international
C. disco also
D. got to
E. band perform

Answer:

14) Find the number that best complete the series. Fill in the missing blank with one of the following options and write your answer below:

7 cars, 15 bicycles, 31 cars, 63 bicycles, ___

A. 165 bicycles
B. 127 cars
C. 92 cars
D. 106 cars
E. 133 bicyles

Answer:

15) Read the information provided and choose the single best answer for the question. Write your answer below:

Rachel is having a party on December 30th, Bill's party is 3 days later, but Rahul is having his a week before Rachel.

What date is Bill's party on?

A. December 29th
B. December 31st
C. January 1st
D. January 2nd
E. January 3rd

Answer:

16) The words in brackets are formed from the main word. Identify the pattern to work out the missing word from the options given. Write your answer below:

Gamer (ram), logic (cog), match (?)

A. MAT
B. MCH
C. TAM
D. MAH
E. HAT

Answer:

17) Select the word from the brackets that will complete the sentence in the most sensible way. Write your answer below:

Bedroom is to SLEEP as kitchen is to (exercise, clean, cook)

Answer:

18) Find one word from each group that together makes one correctly spelt word. The letters must not be rearranged. The word from the first group must always be used first. Write your answer below:

My (great, grand, big) (uncle, mother, sister) always bakes the best cookies!

A. Greatuncle
B. Grandsister
C. Grandmother
D. Greatmother
E. Bigsister

Answer:

19) Find the pair of letters that will continue the series. The alphabet is provided below to help you. Write your answer below:

A B C D E F G H I J K L M N O P Q R S T U V W X Y Z

PS, OU, NW, MY, LA, ___?

Answer:

20) Find the pair of letters that will complete the sentence in the best way. The alphabet is provided below to help you. Write your answer below:

A B C D E F G H I J K L M N O P Q R S T U V W X Y Z

RA is to TD as FY is to ___?

Answer:

Verbal Reasoning - Test 20

21) Select the pair of words, one from each group that are most opposite in meaning to each other from the options given below. Write your answer below:

The opposite of (Take, Throw, Adventure) is (Have, Give, Grab).

A. Throw Give
B. Adventure Grab
C. Throw Have
D. Take Give
E. Take Grab

Answer:

22) Three consecutive letters have been taken out of a word. Select which three letters have been omitted from the options. Write your answer below:

The pair of cows took shelter under the S____E of a nearby tree.

A. HIP
B. HOP
C. HAT
D. HID
E. HAD

Answer:

23) You are required to move one letter from the first word to the second word, creating two new words. Write your answer below:

SHAKE ARC

Answer:

24) Work out the relationship between the word and the code to solve the code and write your answer below:

A B C D E F G H I J K L M N O P Q R S T U V W X Y Z

BOT is to APS. What is the code for PHONE?

Answer:

25) Work out the relationship between the word and the code to solve the code and write your answer below:

A B C D E F G H I J K L M N O P Q R S T U V W X Y Z

BOT is to APS. Decode the following words: ABFT?

Answer:

26) Using the provided code, complete the following sums writing your answer in numbers:

a = 11, b = 1, c = 4, d = 5, e = 6

Solve: a + c − e × b =__?

Answer:

27) Using the provided code, complete the following sums writing your answer in numbers:

a = 11, b = 1, c = 4, d = 5, e = 6

Solve: a − b + c − d =__?

Answer:

28) Write the letter that will complete the word in front of the brackets and begin the word after the brackets. The SAME letter must fit into BOTH sets of brackets. Write your answer below:

mis (_) eal, pas (_) ilk

Answer:

29) Select the two words inside the brackets that are connected in some way to the words outside the brackets. Write your answer below:

CHICKEN PORK (lettuce, beetroot, lamb, turkey, tomato)

Answer:

30) Select the pair of words, one from each group that are most opposite in meaning to each other from the options given. Write your answer below:

The opposite of (Abolish Create Draw) is (Uphold Destroy Try)

A. Abolish Try
B. Draw Try
C. Abolish Uphold
D. Create Uphold
E. Draw Destroy

Answer:

Verbal Reasoning

Verbal Reasoning - Test 20

31) Select the TWO odd words from the options given. Write your answer below:

Cloud, rain, sleet, winter, drizzle

A. Cloud sleet
B. Cloud winter
C. Drizzle sleet
D. Rain winter
E. Rain drizzle

Answer:

32) In each set of numbers, the number in the brackets is related to the two numbers either side of it. Find this relation to work out the missing number '(?)' in the third set. Choose one of the options and write your answer below:

13 (4) 9, 34 (18) 16, 19 (?) 4

A. 15
B. 13
C. 10
D. 4
E. 6

Answer:

33) In each set of numbers, the number in the brackets is related to the two numbers either side of it. Find this relation to work out the missing number '(?)' in the third set. Choose one of the option and write your answer below:

26 (12) 14, 23 (20) 3, 28 (?) 18

A. 21
B. 4
C. 16
D. 19
E. 10

Answer:

34) Find the number that best complete the series. Fill in the missing blank with one of the following options and write your answer below:

4, 6, 10, 18, ___

A. 27
B. 30
C. 19
D. 42
E. 34

Answer:

35) Select the TWO odd words from the options given. Write your answer below:

Quaver, orchestra, music, minim, crochet

A. Orchestra minim
B. Minim crochet
C. Quaver minim
D. Orchestra music
E. Music crochet

Answer:

36) Choose the correct answer by completing the following functions and sums with the correct numbers and signs as appropriate. Write your answer below:

___ ÷ 8 × 6 + 3 = 57

A. 64
B. 72
C. 80
D. 88
E. 96

Answer:

37) Choose the correct answer for the following problem. Write your answer below:

Shan and Jane buy a packet of sweets and two packets of crisps for £1.05. A packet of sweets and one packet of crisps costs 75p. How much is a packet of sweets?

A. 45p
B. 50p
C. 55p
D. 60p
E. 65p

Answer:

38) The words in brackets are formed from the main word. Identify the pattern to work out the missing word from the options given. Write your answer below:

Mates (sat), meals (sea), peaches (?)

A. PEA
B. CEP
C. PES
D. HAP
E. SEA

Answer:

39) Three consecutive letters are removed from the word in CAPITALS. These letters make a word. From the options, find the missing letters to complete the sentence. Write your answer below:

Balraj SCCHED the table by accident.

A. RAM
B. RAP
C. RAT
D. ROT
E. RAN

Answer:

40) Three consecutive letters are removed from the word in CAPITALS. These letters make a word. From the options, find the missing letters to complete the sentence. Write your answer below:

Bernard has a DISCT voice.

A. TAN
B. TAB
C. BIN
D. TIN
E. BAN

Answer:

Verbal Reasoning - Test 21

Time allowed for this paper : 60 minutes

Instructions for Best Practice:

> Attempt all of the questions.
> Ensure that your answers are clearly marked in the answer boxes.
> Calculators and rulers must not be used.
> Equipment recommended: 2 x Pencil & 1 x Eraser.

Verbal Reasoning - Test 21

1) Three consecutive letters are removed from the word in CAPITALS. These letters make a word. From the options, find the missing letters to complete the sentence. Write your answer below:

   Payal chose the DECOION for her party.

   A. RAM
   B. RAN
   C. BAN
   D. RAT
   E. BAT

   Answer:

2) In each set of numbers, the number in the brackets is related to the two numbers either side of it. Find this relation to work out the missing number '(?)' in the third set. Choose one of the options and write your answer below:

   25 (12) 13, 27 (14) 13, 27 (?) 20

   A. 3
   B. 4
   C. 8
   D. 7
   E. 9

   Answer:

3) In each set of numbers, the number in the brackets is related to the two numbers either side of it. Find this relation to work out the missing number '(?)' in the third set. Choose one of the option and write your answer below:

   42 (20) 22, 38 (31) 7, 21 (?) 10

   A. 11
   B. 15
   C. 13
   D. 20
   E. 23

   Answer:

4) A four letter word is hidden between two words in the sentence below. These two words are always next to each other, but there may be punctuation between them. Find this four letter word from one of the options. Write your answer below:

   Morocco really is a fantastic place for a holiday!

   A. a fantastic
   B. a holiday
   C. really is
   D. morocco really
   E. fantastic place

   Answer:

5) A four letter word is hidden between two words in the sentence below. These two words are always next to each other, but there may be punctuation between them. Find this four letter word from one of the options. Write your answer below:

   His agenda tested the patience of even the best organisers.

   A. the patience
   B. the best
   C. best organisers
   D. agenda tested
   E. patience of

   Answer:

6) Find the number that best complete the series. Fill in the missing blank with one of the following options and write your answer below:

   14, 7, 28, 14, 42, __

   A. 30
   B. 21
   C. 56
   D. 7
   E. 14

   Answer:

7) Find the pair of letters that will continue the series. The alphabet is provided below to help you. Write your answer below:

   A B C D E F G H I J K L M N O P Q R S T U V W X Y Z

   ME, KG, II, GK, EM, __?

   Answer:

8) Find the pair of letters that will complete the sentence in the best way. The alphabet is provided below to help you. Write your answer below:

   A B C D E F G H I J K L M N O P Q R S T U V W X Y Z

   KS is to MP as DK is to __?

   Answer:

9) Work out the relationship between the word and the code to solve the code and write your answer below:

   A B C D E F G H I J K L M N O P Q R S T U V W X Y Z

   BOT is to APS. Decode the following: BPMDDBKFQ

   Answer:

10) Work out the relationship between the word and the code to solve the code and write your answer below:

    A B C D E F G H I J K L M N O P Q R S T U V W X Y Z

    BOT is to APS. Decode the following: DZDCQPVT

    Answer:

Verbal Reasoning

© Copyright - Secondary Entrance. All Rights Reserved.

Verbal Reasoning - Test 21

Marks

11) Using the provided code, complete the following sums writing your answer in numbers:

apricot = 7, blueberry = 3, carrot = 2, date = 8, eggplant = 1

Solve: apricot – blueberry × carrot =___?

Answer:

12) Using the provided code, complete the following sums writing your answer in numbers:

apricot = 7, blueberry = 3, carrot = 2, date = 8, eggplant = 1

Solve: date ÷ carrot + blueberry = ___?

Answer:

13) Write the letter that will complete the word in front of the brackets and begin the word after the brackets. The SAME letter must fit into BOTH sets of brackets. Write your answer below:

soc (_) iss, lic (_) ale

Answer:

14) Three consecutive letters have been taken out of a word. Select which three letters have been omitted from the options. Write your answer below:

She placed a lot of S___POO on her hair to ensure it was clean.

A. HIM
B. HAM
C. HUT
D. BUT
E. PUT

Answer:

15) Choose the correct answer for the following problem. Write your answer below:

Share 36 bananas among Patrick, Amir and Sarah in such a way that for every 3 bananas Patrick gets, Sarah gets 2 and Amir gets 4.

How many bananas does Amir get?

A. 15   D. 18
B. 16   E. 19
C. 17

Answer:

16) Read the information provided and choose the single best answer for the question. Write your answer below:

Rachel is having a party on December 30th, Bill's party is 3 days later, but Rahul is having his a week before Rachel.

What date is Rahul's party on?

A. December 21st
B. December 22nd
C. December 23rd
D. December 24th
E. December 25th

Answer:

17) Read the information provided and choose the single best answer for the question. Write your answer below:

Rachel is having a party on December 30th, Bill's party is 3 days later, but Rahul is having his a week before Rachel. Rachel has to postpone her party for a fortnight. What date is it in now?

A. January 13th   D. January 16th
B. January 14th   E. January 17th
C. January 15th

Answer:

18) The words in brackets are formed from the main word. Identify the pattern to work out the missing word from the options given. Write your answer below:

Borne (bone), beast (best), breed (?)

A. REED
B. BEAD
C. RED
D. BRED
E. DEER

Answer:

19) Select the two words inside the brackets that are connected in some way to the words outside the brackets. Write your answer below:

ORANGE BANANA (bread, beetroot, apple, plum, onion)

Answer:

20) Select the word from the brackets that will complete the sentence in the most sensible way. Write your answer below:

Metre is to DISTANCE as ounce is to (weight, time, length)

Answer:

Verbal Reasoning - Test 21

21) Select the TWO odd words from the options given. Write your answer below:

Christian, Arab, Hindu, Muslim, British

A. British Hindu
B. Arab Muslim
C. Arab British
D. Christian Hindu
E. British Muslim

Answer:

22) Choose the correct answer by completing the following functions and sums with the correct numbers and signs as appropriate. Write your answer below:

9 + 8 ÷ ___ + 3 = 39 ÷ 3

A. 5
B. 1
C. 2
D. 4
E. 8

Answer:

23) Choose the correct answer for the following problem. Write your answer below:

Half of a number is three-quarters of 16. What is twice that number?

A. 36
B. 40
C. 44
D. 48
E. 50

Answer:

24) The words in brackets are formed from the main word. Identify the pattern to work out the missing word from the options given. Write your answer below:

Cheat (chat), coins (cons), duvet (?)

A. DUET
B. VET
C. TUDE
D. DUTE
E. DUVE

Answer:

25) Three consecutive letters are removed from the word in CAPITALS. These letters make a word. From the options, find the missing letters to complete the sentence. Write your answer below:

Ben felt a DISTURCE in the force.

A. BAN
B. BUN
C. BAT
D. CAT
E. CAN

Answer:

26) You are required to move one letter from the first word to the second word, creating two new words. Write your answer below:

SAND ICE.

Answer:

27) Write the letter that will complete the word in front of the brackets and begin the word after the brackets. The SAME letter must fit into BOTH sets of brackets. Write your answer below:

gan (_) ore, ban (_) ate

Answer:

28) Select the two words inside the brackets that are connected in some way to the words outside the brackets. Write your answer below:

BENCH SOFA (park, room, chair, stool, table)

Answer:

29) Select the word from the brackets that will complete the sentence in the most sensible way. Write your answer below:

Air is to BREATHE as water is to (drink, rain, sea)

Answer:

30) Three consecutive letters have been taken out of a word. Select which three letters have been omitted from the options. Write your answer below:

He RE____D the same shirt for the second time this week.

A. HIM
B. USE
C. HUT
D. USS
E. PUT

Answer:

Verbal Reasoning

Verbal Reasoning - Test 21

31) You are required to move one letter from the first word to the second word, creating two new words. Write your answer below:

HARM ANT

Answer:

32) Find one word from each group that together makes one correctly spelt word. The letters must not be rearranged. The word from the first group must always be used first. Write your answer below:

Father spread out his (wide, narrow, broad) (paper, mat, sheet) to read during breakfast.

A. Broadmat
B. Narrowsheet
C. Broadsheet
D. Widepaper
E. Widesheet

Answer:

33) Select the pair of words, one from each group that are most opposite in meaning to each other from the options given. Write your answer below:

The opposite of (Abundance Posture Treasure) is (Find Lack Straight).

A. Posture Straight
B. Treasure Find
C. Treasure Lack
D. Abundance Lack
E. Posture Find

Answer:

34) Select the TWO odd words from the options given. Write your answer below:

Comedy, action, book, film, thriller

A. Book film
B. Comedy thriller
C. Comedy film
D. Thriller book
E. Action comedy

Answer:

35) Choose the correct answer by completing the following functions and sums with the correct numbers and signs as appropriate. Write your answer below:

(76 + ___) ÷ 8 ÷ 5 = 2

A. 12
B. 8
C. 16
D. 20
E. 4

Answer:

36) Find the number that best complete the series. Fill in the missing blank with one of the following options and write your answer below:

12 puppets, 6 dolls, 24 puppets, 12 dolls, 36 puppets, ___ dolls.

A. 18
B. 36
C. 24
D. 42
E. 12

Answer:

37) Find one word from each group that together makes one correctly spelt word. The letters must not be rearranged. The word from the first group must always be used first. Write your answer below:

The (sky, air, sea) (port, pier, park) was particularly busy today.

A. Skyport
B. Seapier
C. Airport
D. Seapark
E. Skypark

Answer:

38) Find the pair of letters that will continue the series. The alphabet is provided below to help you. Write your answer below:

A B C D E F G H I J K L M N O P Q R S T U V W X Y Z

HA, IB, JC, KD, LE, ___?

Answer:

39) Find the pair of letters that will complete the sentence in the best way. The alphabet is provided below to help you. Write your answer below:

A B C D E F G H I J K L M N O P Q R S T U V W X Y Z

MI is to KK as PT is to ___?

Answer:

40) Select the pair of words, one from each group that are most opposite in meaning to each other from the options given below. Write your answer below:

The opposite of (Above Fall Trust) is (Within Feel Below).

A. Fall Within
B. Above Below
C. Below Fall
D. Feel Trust
E. Above Feel

Answer:

Verbal Reasoning - Test 22

Time allowed for this paper : 60 minutes

Instructions for Best Practice:

> Attempt all of the questions.
> Ensure that your answers are clearly marked in the answer boxes.
> Calculators and rulers must not be used.
> Equipment recommended: 2 x Pencil & 1 x Eraser.

Verbal Reasoning - Test 22

1) Using the provided code, complete the following sums writing your answer in numbers:

   a = 7, b = 3, c = 2, d = 8, e = 1

   Solve: a − b + e = ___?

   Answer:

2) Using the provided code, complete the following sums writing your answer in numbers:

   a = 7, b = 3, c = 2, d = 8, e = 1

   Solve: a − c ÷ e + b = ___?

   Answer:

3) Write the letter that will complete the word in front of the brackets and begin the word after the brackets. The SAME letter must fit into BOTH sets of brackets. Write your answer below:

   tom (_) elt, wom (_) ank

   Answer:

4) Find the pair of letters that will complete the sentence in the best way. The alphabet is provided below to help you. Write your answer below:

   A B C D E F G H I J K L M N O P Q R S T U V W X Y Z

   GQ is to ET as HT is to ___?

   Answer:

5) Select the pair of words, one from each group that are most opposite in meaning to each other from the options given below. Write your answer below:

   The opposite of (Accept, Worthy, Trust) is (Gather, Refuse, Find).

   A. Accept Refuse
   B. Worthy Refuse
   C. Gather Worthy
   D. Trust Find
   E. Accept Find

   Answer:

6) The words in brackets are formed from the main word. Identify the pattern to work out the missing word from the options given. Write your answer below:

   Hoist (host), lines (lies), titre (?)

   A. TIE
   B. TIRE
   C. TREI
   D. TRIE
   E. RITE

   Answer:

7) Three consecutive letters are removed from the word in CAPITALS. These letters make a word. From the options, find the missing letters to complete the sentence. Write your answer below:

   Roshni was planning the SING for the show.

   A. TIG
   B. TAN
   C. TAP
   D. TIP
   E. TAG

   Answer:

8) Find the number that best complete the series. Fill in the missing blank with one of the following options and write your answer below:

   48, 12, 36, 6, 24, 1, ___

   A. 0
   B. 12
   C. 18
   D. 6
   E. 3

   Answer:

9) Find the pair of letters and numbers that will continue the series. The alphabet is provided below to help you. Write your answer below:

   A B C D E F G H I J K L M N O P Q R S T U V W X Y Z

   F1N1, E2P2, D3R3, C4T4, B5V5, ___?

   Answer:

10) Choose the correct answer by completing the following functions and sums with the correct numbers and signs as appropriate. Write your answer below:

    10 + 3 × 3 + 5 = 8 × 4 − (4 × ___)

    A. 2
    B. 3
    C. 5
    D. 4
    E. 6

    Answer:

Verbal Reasoning - Test 22

11) Find one word from each group that together makes one correctly spelt word. The letters must not be rearranged. The word from the first group must always be used first. Write your answer below:

What a day to go to a (water, sea, ocean) (play, park, boat)!

A. Seapark
B. Oceanboat
C. Waterplay
D. Seaboat
E. Waterpark

Answer:

12) Find the pair of letters that will continue the series. The alphabet is provided below to help you. Write your answer below:

A B C D E F G H I J K L M N O P Q R S T U V W X Y Z

HI, IJ, KL, NO, RS, ___?

Answer:

13) Read the information provided and choose the single best answer for the question. Write your answer below:

3 years ago, Sandeep was 5 and his mother was 7 times his age.

How old will his mother be in 4 years' time?

A. 38   D. 42
B. 40   E. 44
C. 41

Answer:

14) Read the information provided and choose the single best answer for the question. Write your answer below:

3 years ago, Sandeep was 5 and his mother was 7 times his age.

How old will Sandeep be in four years' time?

A. 8   D. 11
B. 9   E. 12
C. 10

Answer:

15) In each set of numbers, the number in the brackets is related to the two numbers either side of it. Find this relation to work out the missing number '(?)' in the third set. Choose one of the options and write your answer below:

4 (2) 2, 16 (2) 14, 17 (?) 13

A. 23
B. 24
C. 4
D. 15
E. 6

Answer:

16) In each set of numbers, the number in the brackets is related to the two numbers either side of it. Find this relation to work out the missing number '(?)' in the third set. Choose one of the option and write your answer below:

18 (3) 15, 12 (7) 5, 14 (?) 3

A. 23
B. 13
C. 21
D. 20
E. 11

Answer:

17) A four letter word is hidden between two words in the sentence below. These two words are always next to each other, but there may be punctuation between them. Find this four letter word from one of the options. Write your answer below:

What do those tortillas taste like?

A. what do
B. taste like
C. do those
D. tortillas taste
E. those tortillas

Answer:

18) A four letter word is hidden between two words in the sentence below. These two words are always next to each other, but there may be punctuation between them. Find this four letter word from one of the options. Write your answer below:

Propaganda terrifies people into doing and believing things that may not be true.

A. terrifies people
B. propaganda terrifies
C. and believing
D. doing and
E. people into

Answer:

19) Write the letter that will complete the word in front of the brackets and begin the word after the brackets. The SAME letter must fit into BOTH sets of brackets. Write your answer below:

lar (_) ish, har (_) eem

Answer:

20) Select the two words inside the brackets that are connected in some way to the words outside the brackets. Write your answer below:

FORK KNIFE (spoon, plate, candle, table, chair)

Answer:

Verbal Reasoning – Test 22

21) Work out the relationship between the word and the code to solve the code and write your answer below:

A B C D E F G H I J K L M N O P Q R S T U V W X Y Z

LAWN is to MBXO. What is the code for FLOWER?

Answer:

22) Work out the relationship between the word and the code to solve the code and write your answer below:

A B C D E F G H I J K L M N O P Q R S T U V W X Y Z

LAWN is to MBXO. What is the code for TREE?

Answer:

23) Select the two words inside the brackets that are connected in some way to the words outside the brackets. Write your answer below:

LAKE RIVER (park, ocean, stream, tree, grass)

Answer:

24) Three consecutive letters have been taken out of a word. Select which three letters have been omitted from the options. Write your answer below:

My favourite B___D of cereal has all been eaten.

A. RUN
B. RAT
C. CAN
D. RAN
E. CAT

Answer:

25) You are required to move one letter from the first word to the second word, creating two new words. Write your answer below:

PATIENT RAN.

Answer:

26) Select the word from the brackets that will complete the sentence in the most sensible way. Write your answer below:

Up is to SKY as Down is to (ground, direction, sad)

Answer:

27) Select the pair of words, one from each group that are most opposite in meaning to each other from the options given. Write your answer below:

The opposite of (Admit Entry Part) is (Gain Deny Feel).

A. Part Gain
B. Admit Gain
C. Part Gain
D. Admit Deny
E. Entry Gain

Answer:

28) Select the TWO odd words from the options given. Write your answer below:

Hospital, doctor, dentist, office, optician

A. Hospital doctor
B. Optician office
C. Dentist doctor
D. Hospital office
E. Hospital dentist

Answer:

29) Choose the correct answer by completing the following functions and sums with the correct numbers and signs as appropriate. Write your answer below:

67 + (9 × ___) = 11 × 11

A. 2
B. 5
C. 6
D. 9
E. 7

Answer:

30) Choose the correct answer for the following problem. Write your answer below:

Half of a number added to 15 is 7 less than 28. What is the number?

A. 10
B. 12
C. 14
D. 16
E. 18

Answer:

Verbal Reasoning - Test 22

31) Choose the correct answer for the following problem. Write your answer below:

A pencil costs twice as much as a rubber. Two pencils and a rubber cost 75p. How much is a rubber?

A. 5p
B. 10p
C. 15p
D. 20p
E. 25p

Answer:

32) The words in brackets are formed from the main word. Identify the pattern to work out the missing word from the options given. Write your answer below:

Feast (fest), gleam (glam), cream (?)

A. REAM
B. MEAR
C. RAME
D. CRAM
E. CREM

Answer:

33) Three consecutive letters are removed from the word in CAPITALS. These letters make a word. From the options, find the missing letters to complete the sentence. Write your answer below:

Bruce's job needed him to be very VERILE.

A. TAP
B. SIT
C. SUM
D. SAT
E. SIP

Answer:

34) Find the number that best complete the series. Fill in the missing blank with one of the following options and write your answer below:

1250, 250, 50, 10, ___

A. 5
B. 1
C. 2
D. 4
E. 0

Answer:

35) Three consecutive letters have been taken out of a word. Select which three letters have been omitted from the options. Write your answer below:

The artist attempted to TR___ out the silhouette with amazing precision.

A. ACE
B. EAR
C. ONE
D. ALL
E. ART

Answer:

36) You are required to move one letter from the first word to the second word, creating two new words. Write your answer below:

CRAB CANE.

Answer:

37) Select the word from the brackets that will complete the sentence in the most sensible way. Write your answer below:

Morning is to BREAKFAST as evening is to (break, lunch, dinner)

Answer:

38) Find one word from each group that together makes one correctly spelt word. The letters must not be rearranged. The word from the first group must always be used first. Write your answer below:

He woke up just at (day, noon, night) (tear, rip, break).

A. Daybreak
B. Noonrip
C. Nightear
D. Noonbreak
E. Dayrip

Answer:

39) Find the pair of letters that will complete the sentence in the best way. The alphabet is provided below to help you. Write your answer below:

A B C D E F G H I J K L M N O P Q R S T U V W X Y Z

IL is to JK as KN is to ___?

Answer:

40) Select the TWO odd words from the options given. Write your answer below:

Commence, end, begin, start, finish

A. Commence end
B. Start finish
C. Begin end
D. Start commence
E. End finish

Answer:

Verbal Reasoning - Test 23

Time allowed for this paper : 60 minutes

Instructions for Best Practice:

> Attempt all of the questions.
> Ensure that your answers are clearly marked in the answer boxes.
> Calculators and rulers must not be used.
> Equipment recommended: 2 x Pencil & 1 x Eraser.

Verbal Reasoning - Test 23

1) You are required to move one letter from the first word to the second word, creating **two new words**. Write your answer below:

   BRAND TICK.

   Answer:

2) Work out the relationship between the word and the code to solve the code and write your answer below:

   A B C D E F G H I J K L M N O P Q R S T U V W X Y Z

   LAWN is to MBXO. What is the code for GRASS?

   Answer:

3) Work out the relationship between the word and the code to solve the code and write your answer below:

   A B C D E F G H I J K L M N O P Q R S T U V W X Y Z

   LAWN is to MBXO. <u>Decode</u> the following: UVMJQ.

   Answer:

4) Find one word from each group that together makes **one correctly spelt word**. The letters must not be rearranged. The word from the first group **must always** be used first. Write your answer below:

   (sea, ocean, lake) (son, father, brother)

   A. Seafather
   B. Oceanbrother
   C. Lakeson
   D. Lakefather
   E. Season

   Answer:

5) Find the pair of letters that will continue the series. The alphabet is provided below to help you. Write your answer below:

   A B C D E F G H I J K L M N O P Q R S T U V W X Y Z

   OP, NR, LU, IY, ED, ___?

   Answer:

6) Choose the correct answer for the following problem. Write your answer below:

   A rectangle has sides 6 cm and 9 cm which touch to form a right angle. What is the area of the rectangle?

   A. 14 cm^2
   B. 55 cm^2
   C. 56 cm^2
   D. 53 cm^2
   E. 54 cm^2

   Answer:

7) Three consecutive letters are removed from the word in CAPITALS. These letters make a word. From the options, **find the missing letters** to complete the sentence. Write your answer below:

   Kunal CHED on the test.

   A. EEL
   B. EAR
   C. BUS
   D. EAT
   E. EYE

   Answer:

8) In each set of numbers, the number in the brackets is related to the two numbers either side of it. Find this relation to work out the missing number '(?)' in the third set. Choose one of the options and write your answer below:

   24 (2) 22, 19 (4) 15, 18 (?) 12

   A. 6
   B. 18
   C. 22
   D. 16
   E. 15

   Answer:

9) In each set of numbers, the number in the brackets is related to the two numbers either side of it. Find this relation to work out the missing number '(?)' in the third set. Choose one of the options and write your answer below:

   3 (27) 9, 4 (16) 4, 5 (?) 4

   A. 14
   B. 25
   C. 13
   D. 11
   E. 20

   Answer:

10) Find the pair of letters that will complete the sentence in the best way. The alphabet is provided below to help you. Write your answer below:

    A B C D E F G H I J K L M N O P Q R S T U V W X Y Z

    TB is to WD as XH is to ___?

    Answer:

Verbal Reasoning - Test 23

11) Select the pair of words, one from each group that are most opposite in meaning to each other from the options given below. Write your answer below:

The opposite of (Agree, Venture, Indent) is (Handy, Refuse, Tell).

A. Venture Tell
B. Indent Refuse
C. Agree Handy
D. Indent Handy
E. Agree Refuse

Answer:

12) Select the two words inside the brackets that are connected in some way to the words outside the brackets. Write your answer below:

CALF CHICK (cow, horse, lamb, kid, goat)

Answer:

13) Select the word from the brackets that will complete the sentence in the most sensible way. Write your answer below:

Light is to LAMP as sound is to (speaker, noise, volume)

Answer:

14) Choose the correct answer by completing the following functions and sums with the correct numbers and signs as appropriate. Write your answer below:

(108 ÷ 9 × 3) ÷ ___ = 12 − (2 × 3)

A. 1
B. 3
C. 12
D. 9
E. 6

Answer:

15) Choose the correct answer for the following problem. Write your answer below:

A circle can be drawn inside a square so that the circle just touches all 4 sides of the square. If the square has an area of 36 sq. cm, what is the radius of the circle?

A. 3
B. 4
C. 5
D. 6
E. 11

Answer:

16) Read the information provided and choose the single best answer for the question. Write your answer below:

If John had 7 more books, he would have half as many as Raj. John has 15 books.
How many books does Raj have?

A. 38
B. 44
C. 65
D. 52
E. 48

Answer:

17) Three consecutive letters are removed from the word in CAPITALS. These letters make a word. From the options, find the missing letters to complete the sentence. Write your answer below:

Alice climbed the STS up to her bedroom.

A. ASK
B. AIR
C. ARM
D. EAR
E. END

Answer:

18) A four letter word is hidden between two words in the sentence below. These two words are always next to each other, but there may be punctuation between them. Find this four letter word from one of the options. Write your answer below:

Have you seen the new pandas brought in to the zoo?

A. the new
B. brought in
C. seen the
D. pandas brought
E. to the

Answer:

19) A four letter word is hidden between two words in the sentence below. These two words are always next to each other, but there may be punctuation between them. Find this four letter word from one of the options. Write your answer below:

The key to staying healthy is happiness and laughter.

A. staying healthy
B. key to
C. is happiness
D. happiness and
E. and laughter

Answer:

20) Find the number that best complete the series. Fill in the missing blank with one of the following options and write your answer below:

1024, 256, 64, 16, ___

A. 1
B. 4
C. 8
D. 10
E. 16

Answer:

Verbal Reasoning - Test 23

21) Three consecutive letters have been taken out of a word. Select which three letters have been omitted from the options. Write your answer below:

PERFOR___CE

A. BAN
B. CAN
C. MAN
D. CAT
E. MAT

Answer:

22) You are required to move one letter from the first word to the second word, creating two new words. Write your answer below:

HORSE STAND.

Answer:

23) Using the provided code, complete the following sums writing your answer in numbers:

a = 7, b = 3, c = 2, d = 8, e = 1

Solve: c + a − b × e = ___?

Answer:

24) Write the letter that will complete the word in front of the brackets and begin the word after the brackets. The SAME letter must fit into BOTH sets of brackets. Write your answer below:

kee (_) ose, lea (_) ice

Answer:

25) Find one word from each group that together makes one correctly spelt word. The letters must not be rearranged. The word from the first group must always be used first. Write your answer below:

The children loved playing in the (play, fun, joy) (floor, ground, flat) by the park.

A. Playfloor
B. Playground
C. Joyflat
D. Funfloor
E. Funground

Answer:

26) Find the pair of letters that will continue the series. The alphabet is provided below to help you. Write your answer below:

A B C D E F G H I J K L M N O P Q R S T U V W X Y Z

PM, QO, SR, VV, ZA, ___?

Answer:

27) The words in brackets are formed from the main word. Identify the pattern to work out the missing word from the options given. Write your answer below:

Tones (toes), hoops (hops), pants (?)

A. ANTS
B. TANS
C. TAPS
D. PATS
E. PANS

Answer:

28) Select the word from the brackets that will complete the sentence in the most sensible way. Write your answer below:

Clock is to TIME as tape is to (speed, distance, measure)

Answer:

29) Find the pair of letters that will complete the sentence in the best way. The alphabet is provided below to help you. Write your answer below:

A B C D E F G H I J K L M N O P Q R S T U V W X Y Z

WC is to VB as ZE is to ___?

Answer:

30) Select the pair of words, one from each group that are most opposite in meaning to each other from the options given. Write your answer below:

(Errand Walnut Arrive) (Depart Dessert Joke)

A. Errand Depart
B. Walnut Dessert
C. Dessert Errand
D. Joke Errand
E. Arrive Depart

Answer:

Verbal Reasoning - Test 23

31) Select the TWO odd words from the options given. Write your answer below:

Shop, Cinema, Theatre, Office, Arena

A. Shop cinema
B. Arena office
C. Theatre shop
D. Shop office
E. Cinema Arena

Answer:

32) The words in brackets are formed from the main word. Identify the pattern to work out the missing word from the options given. Write your answer below:

Camera (are), border (red), waffle (?)

A. ALE
B. FLA
C. WEL
D. FEW
E. ELF

Answer:

33) Find the number that best complete the series. Fill in the missing blank with one of the following options and write your answer below:

81, 27, 9, 3, ___

A. 3
B. 9
C. 1
D. 0
E. 6

Answer:

34) Three consecutive letters have been taken out of a word. Select which three letters have been omitted from the options. Write your answer below:

We all had to rush to the HOS___AL as quick as possible.

A. PAT
B. PIT
C. PUT
D. BIT
E. BUT

Answer:

35) Using the provided code, complete the following sums writing your answer in numbers:

a = 3, b = 5, c = 8, d = 12, e = 4

Solve: d − c ÷ e = ___?

Answer:

36) Write the letter that will complete the word in front of the brackets and begin the word after the brackets. The SAME letter must fit into BOTH sets of brackets. Write your answer below:

tal (_) ase, ban (_) cho

Answer:

37) Select the two words inside the brackets that are connected in some way to the words outside the brackets. Write your answer below:

COAT SHIRT (bag, ring, shorts, shoes, feet)

Answer:

38) Select the TWO odd words from the options given. Write your answer below:

Pop, ballroom, bedroom, ballet, salsa

A. Ballroom bedroom
B. Pop bedroom
C. Ballet pop
D. Salsa ballroom
E. Bedroom ballet

Answer:

39) Choose the correct answer by completing the following functions and sums with the correct numbers and signs as appropriate. Write your answer below:

156 = 7 × 12 + ___ × 6

A. 5
B. 7
C. 8
D. 12
E. 4

Answer:

40) Read the information provided and choose the single best answer for the question. Write your answer below:

Lisa was 3 when her brother was born and her mum was 10 times as old as she was. When Lisa's mum is 50 years old, how old will her brother be?

A. 17
B. 18
C. 19
D. 20
E. 21

Answer:

Verbal Reasoning - Test 24

Time allowed for this paper : 60 minutes

Instructions for Best Practice:

> Attempt all of the questions.
> Ensure that your answers are clearly marked in the answer boxes.
> Calculators and rulers must not be used.
> Equipment recommended: 2 x Pencil & 1 x Eraser.

Verbal Reasoning - Test 24

1) Work out the relationship between the word and the code to solve the code and write your answer below:

   A B C D E F G H I J K L M N O P Q R S T U V W X Y Z

   LAWN is to MBXO. Decode the following: TPJM?

   Answer:

2) Work out the relationship between the word and the code to solve the code and write your answer below:

   A B C D E F G H I J K L M N O P Q R S T U V W X Y Z

   LAWN is to MBXO. Decode the following: MFBWFT?

   Answer:

3) Using the provided code, complete the following sums writing your answer in numbers:

   aa = 3, bb = 5, cc = 8, dd = 12, ee = 4

   Solve: aa + bb − cc = __?

   Answer:

4) Using the provided code, complete the following sums writing your answer in numbers:

   a = 3, b = 5, c = 8, d = 12, e = 4

   Solve: d − e × a = __?

   Answer:

5) Write the letter that will complete the word in front of the brackets and begin the word after the brackets. The SAME letter must fit into BOTH sets of brackets. Write your answer below:

   sto (_) ost, pum (_) ick

   Answer:

6) Select the TWO odd words from the options given. Write your answer below:

   Car, bicycle, unicycle, van, lorry, truck

   A. Car lorry
   B. Bicycle unicycle
   C. Car lorry
   D. Car bicycle
   E. Unicycle van

   Answer:

7) Choose the correct answer for the following problem. Write your answer below:

   Jim has 3 times as much money as Fiona who is 12p short of 30p. How much money does Jim have?

   A. 54p
   B. 57p
   C. 60p
   D. 63p
   E. 66p

   Answer:

8) Read the information provided and choose the single best answer for the question. Write your answer below:

   In 2 years' time, Ross will be 3 times as old as his sister will be then. His sister is now 2. When Ross is 13, how old will his sister be?

   A. 5
   B. 6
   C. 7
   D. 8
   E. 9

   Answer:

9) In each set of numbers, the number in the brackets is related to the two numbers either side of it. Find this relation to work out the missing number '(?)' in the third set. Choose one of the options and write your answer below:

   15 (30) 2, 21 (42) 2, 17 (?) 2

   A. 11
   B. 17
   C. 34
   D. 15
   E. 14

   Answer:

10) In each set of numbers, the number in the brackets is related to the two numbers either side of it. Find this relation to work out the missing number '(?)' in the third set. Choose one of the option and write your answer below:

    1 (4) 4, 3 (12) 4, 5 (20) ?

    A. 17
    B. 4
    C. 14
    D. 24
    E. 7

    Answer:

Verbal Reasoning - Test 24

11) Select the pair of words, one from each group that are most opposite in meaning to each other from the options given. Write your answer below:

The opposite of (Neck Near Narrow) is (Winter Wool Wide).

A. Near Wide
B. Narrow Wide
C. Winter Near
D. Neck Wool
E. Narrow Winter

Answer:

12) Select the **TWO odd words** from the options given. Write your answer below:

Baker, greengrocer, butcher, shop, worker

A. Baker shop
B. Butcher worker
C. Shop worker
D. Greengrocer baker
E. Worker baker

Answer:

13) Select the word from the brackets that will complete the sentence in the most sensible way. Write your answer below:

Winter is to COLD as summer is to (windy, hot, rain)

Answer:

14) Find one word from each group that together makes one correctly spelt word. The letters must not be rearranged. The word from the first group must always be used first. Write your answer below:

The pair of them were sent to the (head, hair, nose) (master, boss, lead).

A. Hairmaster   D. Headmaster
B. Headboss   E. Noselead
C. Noseboss

Answer:

15) Choose the correct answer by completing the following functions and sums with the correct numbers and signs as appropriate. Write your answer below:

77 + 11 ÷ 11 = ___ + 4

A. 71
B. 74
C. 53
D. 67
E. 62

Answer:

16) Choose the correct answer for the following problem. Write your answer below:

One third of a certain number is the same as one fifth of forty-five. What is the number?

A. 24
B. 27
C. 30
D. 33
E. 36

Answer:

17) Read the information provided and choose the single best answer for the question. Write your answer below:

The Jones family live two houses away from the Yus family on the same side of the road. The Jones family are at the end of the road at house number 38. The Jones family are on the side of the road with even numbers.

What is the house number of the Yus family?

A. 33   D. 36
B. 34   E. 37
C. 35

Answer:

18) The words in brackets are formed from the main word. Identify the pattern to work out the missing word from the options given. Write your answer below:

Jersey (yes), wonder (red), kimonos (?)

A. SON
B. NOM
C. KIM
D. KON
E. MON

Answer:

19) A four letter word is hidden between two words in the sentence below. These two words are always next to each other, but there may be punctuation between them. Find this four letter word from one of the options. Write your answer below:

A marmalade advert has just been made better!

A. A marmalade
B. advert has
C. has just
D. marmalade advert
E. been made

Answer:

20) A four letter word is hidden between two words in the sentence below. These two words are always next to each other, but there may be punctuation between them. Find this four letter word from one of the options. Write your answer below:

Do you have a portable adaptor for a phone charger?

A. you have
B. phone charger
C. adaptor for
D. portable adaptor
E. a portable

Answer:

Verbal Reasoning - Test 24

21) Find the **number** that best complete the series. Fill in the **missing blank** with one of the following options and write your answer below:

28, 4, 21, 8, 14, 12, ___

A. 6
B. 12
C. 7
D. 14
E. 3

Answer:

22) You are required to move one letter from the first word to the second word, creating two **new words**. Write your answer below:

RACE ATE.

Answer:

23) Write the letter that will **complete the word** in front of the **brackets** and begin the word after the brackets. The SAME letter must fit into BOTH sets of brackets. Write your answer below:

sui (_) ime, pas (_) omb

Answer:

24) Select the two words **inside the brackets** that are connected in some way to the words **outside the brackets**. Write your answer below:

HOUSE FLAT (car, bus, lorry, apartment, bungalow)

Answer:

25) Find the **pair of letters** that will continue the series. The alphabet is provided below to help you. Write your answer below:

A B C D E F G H I J K L M N O P Q R S T U V W X Y Z

AM, BN, CO, DP, EQ, ___ ?

Answer:

26) Find the **pair of letters** that will complete the sentence in the best way. The alphabet is provided below to help you. Write your answer below:

A B C D E F G H I J K L M N O P Q R S T U V W X Y Z

XX is to YZ as FF is to ___?

Answer:

27) Choose the correct answer by **completing the following functions and sums** with the **correct numbers and signs** as appropriate. Write your answer below:

23 × 2 = 56 + 4 − ___

A. 35
B. 24
C. 17
D. 44
E. 14

Answer:

28) The words in brackets are formed from the main word. **Identify the pattern** to work out the **missing word** from the options given. Write your answer below:

Debris (sir), corridor (rod), until (?)

A. TIN
B. LIT
C. TUN
D. NUT
E. NUL

Answer:

29) Three consecutive letters are removed from the word in CAPITALS. These letters make a word. From the options, find the **missing letters** to complete the sentence. Write your answer below:

Kate wrote the SCT for the play.

A. RUN
B. RAM
C. RIP
D. RAN
E. RAT

Answer:

30) Three consecutive letters have been taken out of a word. Select which three letters **have been omitted** from the options. Write your answer below:

The victor stood at the ___IUM.

A. PIT
B. PAD
C. PAT
D. POD
E. POT

Answer:

Verbal Reasoning - Test 24

31) You are required to move one letter from the first word to the second word, creating **two new words**. These can be used to complete the sentence.

AROUND ROD.
"A roundabout could be called a _____ _____ I suppose?" pondered George to himself.

Answer:

32) Select the two words **inside the brackets** that are connected in some way to the words **outside the brackets**. Write your answer below:

FALCON EAGLE (pigeon, hen, vulture, hawk, robin)

Answer:

33) Select the word from the brackets that will **complete the sentence in the most sensible way**. Write your answer below:

Tennis is to COURT as football is to (pitch, arena, square)

Answer:

34) Find one word **from each group** that together makes **one correctly spelt word**. The letters **must not be rearranged**. The word from the first group **must always** be used first. Write your answer below:

I am going to the (green, red, blue) (grocer, butcher, baker) to buy some fresh food.

A. Redbutcher   D. Greenbutcher
B. Bluebaker   E. Redgrocer
C. Greengrocer

Answer:

35) Find the pair of letters that will continue the series. The alphabet is provided below to help you. Write your answer below:

A B C D E F G H I J K L M N O P Q R S T U V W X Y Z

TV, ST, RR, QP, PN, ___?

Answer:

36) Find the number that best complete the series. Fill in the missing blank with one of the following options and write your answer below:

243, 81, 27, 9, ___

A. 1
B. 9
C. 18
D. 6
E. 3

Answer:

37) Three consecutive letters have been taken out of a word. Select which three letters **have been omitted** from the options. Write your answer below:

I hope to have a good ___EER in the future.

A. BAR
B. CAR
C. EAR
D. FAR
E. TAR

Answer:

38) Find the pair of letters that will complete the sentence in the best way. The alphabet is provided below to help you. Write your answer below:

A B C D E F G H I J K L M N O P Q R S T U V W X Y Z

HK is to EN as OR is to ___?

Answer:

39) Select the pair of words, one from each group that are most opposite in meaning to each other from the options given below. Write your answer below:

The opposite of (Cloth, Truce, Back) is (Disaster, Model, Front).

A. Truce Model
B. Back Disaster
C. Cloth Front
D. Truce Disaster
E. Back Front

Answer:

40) Three consecutive letters are removed from the word in CAPITALS. These letters make a word. From the options, find the missing letters to complete the sentence. Write your answer below:

Gordon sets TS for the mice.

A. AXE
B. RIP
C. RAN
D. RUN
E. RAP

Answer:

Verbal Reasoning - Test 25

Time allowed for this paper : 60 minutes

Instructions for Best Practice:

> Attempt all of the questions.
> Ensure that your answers are clearly marked in the answer boxes.
> Calculators and rulers must not be used.
> Equipment recommended: 2 x Pencil & 1 x Eraser.

Verbal Reasoning - Test 25

1) Write the letter that will complete the word in front of the brackets and begin the word after the brackets. The SAME letter must fit into BOTH sets of brackets. Write your answer below:

   tam (_) ast, har (_) mit

   Answer:

2) Select the two words inside the brackets that are connected in some way to the words outside the brackets. Write your answer below:

   Ray only likes certain types of sports. He likes RACQUETBALL, BADMINTON (dodgeball, rugby, tennis, squash, netball)

   Answer:

3) Find one word from each group that together makes one correctly spelt word. The letters must not be rearranged. The word from the first group must always be used first. Write your answer below:

   Simon put his book back onto the (magazine, paper, book) (shelf, area, room).

   A. Paperarea   D. Paperroom
   B. Magazineshelf E. Bookroom
   C. Bookshelf

   Answer:

4) Find the pair of letters that will continue the series. The alphabet is provided below to help you. Write your answer below:

   A B C D E F G H I J K L M N O P Q R S T U V W X Y Z

   PB, ___, RZ, SY, TX, UW?

   Answer:

5) Choose the correct answer for the following problem. Write your answer below:

   Harman, who will be 5 next year, is 2 years younger than Kabir. How old is Kabir now?

   A. 9
   B. 8
   C. 7
   D. 6
   E. 5

   Answer:

6) Read the information provided and choose the single best answer for the question. Write your answer below:

   Ajay, Sanjana and Calvin wore blue jeans.
   Sanjana, Calvin and Dom wore grey jumpers.
   Dom, Sam and Nathan wore red shorts.
   Ajay and Nathan wore navy jumpers.

   Who wore red shorts and a navy jumper?

   A. Calvin   D. Sam
   B. Dom   E. Ajay
   C. Nathan

   Answer:

7) Read the information provided and choose the single best answer for the question. Write your answer below:

   Ajay, Sanjana and Calvin wore blue jeans.
   Sanjana and Dom wore grey jumpers.
   Dom, Sam and Nathan wore red shorts.
   Ajay and Nathan wore navy jumpers.

   Who wore a grey jumper and blue jeans?
   A. Ajay
   B. Sanjana
   C. Calvin
   D. Dom
   E. Nathan

   Answer:

8) The words in brackets are formed from the main word. Identify the pattern to work out the missing word from the options given. Write your answer below:

   Magnet (ten), fasten (net), hostel (?)

   A. LOT
   B. SOT
   C. HOT
   D. HET
   E. LET

   Answer:

9) Choose the correct answer by completing the following functions and sums with the correct numbers and signs as appropriate. Write your answer below:

   (31 − 6 + 5) ÷ 3 = 4 + 4 × ___ + 2

   A. 1
   B. 2
   C. 3
   D. 4
   E. 5

   Answer:

10) Choose the correct answer for the following problem. Write your answer below:

    Six times a number is four more than quadruple 11. What is the number?

    A. 5
    B. 6
    C. 7
    D. 8
    E. 9

    Answer:

Verbal Reasoning

Verbal Reasoning - Test 25

11) The words in brackets are formed from the main word. Identify the pattern to work out the missing word from the options given. Write your answer below:

Tortilla (all), cheetah (hat), pupil (?)

A. PIL
B. LIP
C. PUP
D. PIL
E. LUP

Answer:

12) Three consecutive letters are removed from the word in CAPITALS. These letters make a word. From the options, find the missing letters to complete the sentence. Write your answer below:

Morgan made sure he paid his TS in time.

A. ARM
B. HAM
C. EAT
D. AXE
E. HIT

Answer:

13) Using the provided code, complete the following sums writing your answer in numbers:

Aa = 3, Bb = 5, Cc = 8, Dd = 12, Ee = 4

Solve: Bb x Ee − Dd ÷ Aa = ___?

Answer:

14) Using the provided code, complete the following sums writing your answer in numbers:

a = 3, b = 5, c = 8, d = 12, e = 4

Solve: d ÷ e x a + b = ___?

Answer:

15) Write the letter that will complete the word in front of the brackets and begin the word after the brackets. The SAME letter must fit into BOTH sets of brackets. Write your answer below:

ban (_) ame, han (_) one

Answer:

16) Select the two words inside the brackets that are connected in some way to the words outside the brackets. Write your answer below:

We have many senses. These include TASTE, SIGHT (touch, smell, walk, run, swim)

Answer:

17) Three consecutive letters have been taken out of a word. Select which three letters have been omitted from the options. Write your answer below:

Make sure you write out your answers on a blank piece of P___R.

A. ATE
B. ART
C. ARM
D. ARC
E. APE

Answer:

18) Find the pair of letters that will continue the series. The alphabet is provided below to help you. Write your answer below:

A B C D E F G H I J K L M N O P Q R S T U V W X Y Z

DW, FY, HA, JC, LE, ___?

Answer:

19) Find the pair of letters that will complete the sentence in the best way. The alphabet is provided below to help you. Write your answer below:

A B C D E F G H I J K L M N O P Q R S T U V W X Y Z

LU is to KV as GN is to ___?

Answer:

20) Select the TWO odd words from the options given. Write your answer below:

Drive, walk, jog, run, ride

A. Jog ride
B. Drive walk
C. Run ride
D. Drive ride
E. Jog walk

Answer:

Verbal Reasoning - Test 25

21) Choose the correct answer by **completing the following functions and sums** with the **correct numbers and signs** as appropriate. Write your answer below:

17 + 2 × ___ = 6 × 5 − 5

A. 4
B. 6
C. 2
D. 5
E. 8

Answer:

22) You are required to move one letter from the first word to the second word, creating **two new words**. Write your answer below:

SCUM ROOK

Answer:

23) Work out the relationship between the word and the code to solve the code and write your answer below:

A B C D E F G H I J K L M N O P Q R S T U V W X Y Z

Your teacher prepared a codebreaker for you. Can you solve it?

TENNIS is to VCPLKQ. What is the code for HOCKEY?

Answer:

24) Work out the relationship between the word and the code to solve the code and write your answer below:

A B C D E F G H I J K L M N O P Q R S T U V W X Y Z

Your teacher prepared a codebreaker for you. Can you solve it?

TENNIS is to VCPLKQ.

What is the code for CRICKET?

Answer:

25) Select the word from the brackets that will **complete the sentence in the most sensible way**. Write your answer below:

Bike is to RIDE as YACHT is to (sit, sail, drive)

Answer:

26) Select the pair of words, one from each group that are most opposite in meaning to each other from the options given. Write your answer below:

The opposite of (Endanger Jacket Difficult) is (Wild Top Simple).

A. Jacket Top
B. Endanger Simple
C. Difficult Top
D. Endanger Wild
E. Difficult Simple

Answer:

27) Select the **TWO odd words** from the options given. Write your answer below:

High, normal, low, average, usual

A. High average
B. Normal usual
C. Low usual
D. Average normal
E. High low

Answer:

28) Three consecutive letters are removed from the word in CAPITALS. These letters make a word. From the options, find the **missing letters** to complete the sentence. Write your answer below:

It took a long time to DLOAD the movie.

A. OWN
B. OUT
C. OAT
D. ARK
E. AND

Answer:

29) In each set of numbers, the number in the brackets is related to **the two numbers either side of it**. Find this **relation** to work out the missing number '(?)' in the third set. Choose one of the options and write your answer below:

3 (24) 8, 5 (25) 5, 7 (?) 4

A. 7
B. 28
C. 23
D. 10
E. 5

Answer:

30) In each set of numbers, the number in the brackets is related to **the two numbers either side of it**. Find this **relation** to work out the missing number '(?)' in the third set. Choose one of the option and write your answer below:

2 (8) 4, 5 (10) 2, 6 (?) 5

A. 25
B. 21
C. 23
D. 2
E. 30

Answer:

Verbal Reasoning - Test 25

31) A four letter word is hidden between two words in the sentence below. These two words are always next to each other, but there may be punctuation between them. Find this four letter word from one of the options. Write your answer below:

The warden who controlled the water slide admitted only children above the age of 12.

A. only children
B. water slide
C. above the
D. controlled the
E. slide admitted

Answer:

32) Three consecutive letters have been taken out of a word. Select which three letters have been omitted from the options. Write your answer below:

The PELI___ was the main attraction at the zoo.

A. CAB
B. CAT
C. CAN
D. CAR
E. CUB

Answer:

33) You are required to move one letter from the first word to the second word, creating two new words. Write your answer below:

TOWN SAKE

Answer:

34) Select the word from the brackets that will complete the sentence in the most sensible way. Write your answer below:

House is to LIVE as office is to (work, play, sleep)

Answer:

35) Find one word from each group that together makes one correctly spelt word. The letters must not be rearranged. The word from the first group must always be used first. Write your answer below:

The (honey, sugar, nectar) (bee, hornet, wasp) is a rare sight in today's gardens.

A. Sugarbee
B. Nectarhornet
C. Honeywasp
D. Honeybee
E. Sugarwasp

Answer:

36) Find the pair of letters that will complete the sentence in the best way. The alphabet is provided below to help you. Write your answer below:

A B C D E F G H I J K L M N O P Q R S T U V W X Y Z

MJ is to OH as GD is to ___?

Answer:

37) Select the pair of words, one from each group that are most opposite in meaning to each other from the options given below. Write your answer below:

(Denim Thrust Cool) (Fire Tool Warm)

A. Cool Warm
B. Thrust Fire
C. Warm Denim
D. Cool Fire
E. Thrust Tool

Answer:

38) A four letter word is hidden between two words in the sentence below. These two words are always next to each other, but there may be punctuation between them. Find this four letter word from one of the options. Write your answer below:

Becky was in charge of maintenance of the school.

A. charge of
B. in charge
C. maintenance of
D. was in
E. the school

Answer:

39) Find the number that best complete the series. Fill in the missing blank with one of the following options and write your answer below:

8, 4, 2, 1, 2, 4, ___

A. 3
B. 4
C. 8
D. 10
E. 6

Answer:

40) Find the number that best complete the series. Fill in the missing blank with one of the following options and write your answer below:

36, 24, 30, 18, 24, ___

A. 24
B. 12
C. 36
D. 18
E. 6

Answer:

Verbal Reasoning - Test 26

Time allowed for this paper : 60 minutes

Instructions for Best Practice:

> Attempt all of the questions.
> Ensure that your answers are clearly marked in the answer boxes.
> Calculators and rulers must not be used.
> Equipment recommended: 2 x Pencil & 1 x Eraser.

Verbal Reasoning - Test 26

1) Read the information provided and choose the single best answer for the question. Write your answer below:

   Rohan has £5 more than Fiona. Fiona has £5 less than Andy. Tina has £20 which is £2 more than Rohan. How much money does Andy have?

   A. £10
   B. £12
   C. £14
   D. £16
   E. £18

   Answer:

2) The words in brackets are formed from the main word. Identify the pattern to work out the missing word from the options given. Write your answer below:

   Tennis (sin), guitar (rat), democrat (?)

   A. CAR
   B. DAT
   C. RAT
   D. MAT
   E. TAR

   Answer:

3) In each set of numbers, the number in the brackets is related to the two numbers either side of it. Find this relation to work out the missing number '(?)' in the third set. Choose one of the options and write your answer below:

   13 (26) 2, 7 (49) 7, 12 (?) 3

   A. 15
   B. 23
   C. 36
   D. 14
   E. 6

   Answer:

4) In each set of numbers, the number in the brackets is related to the two numbers either side of it. Find this relation to work out the missing number '(?)' in the third set. Choose one of the option and write your answer below:

   21 (63) 3, 15 (45) 3, 9 (?) 11

   A. 78
   B. 84
   C. 42
   D. 31
   E. 99

   Answer:

5) You are required to move one letter from the first word to the second word, creating two new words. Write your answer below:

   SOLDIER GRAN

   Answer:

6) Work out the relationship between the word and the code to solve the code and write your answer below:

   A B C D E F G H I J K L M N O P Q R S T U V W X Y Z

   TENNIS is to VCPLKQ. What is the code for FOOTBALL?

   Answer:

7) Work out the relationship between the word and the code to solve the code and write your answer below:

   A B C D E F G H I J K L M N O P Q R S T U V W X Y Z

   TENNIS is to VCPLKQ. Decode the following: LSFM.

   Answer:

8) Using the provided code, complete the following sums writing your answer in LETTERS:

   a = 1, b = 4, c = 9, d = 6, e = 2

   Solve: b + e = __?

   Answer:

9) Using the provided code, complete the following sums writing your answer in LETTERS:

   a = 1, b = 4, c = 9, d = 6, e = 2

   Solve: e x a = __?

   Answer:

10) Write the letter that will complete the word in front of the brackets and begin the word after the brackets. The SAME letter must fit into BOTH sets of brackets. Write your answer below:

    bal (_) ick, hil (_) ong

    Answer:

Verbal Reasoning - Test 26

11) Three consecutive letters have been taken out of a word. Select which three letters have been omitted from the options. Write your answer below:

He brought much S____E on his family by refusing to fight in the battle.

A. ARK
B. ART
C. ARM
D. HAM
E. HAT

Answer:

12) You are required to move one letter from the first word to the second word, creating two new words. Write your answer below:

THEN TANK

Answer:

13) Find the pair of letters that will complete the sentence in the best way. The alphabet is provided below to help you. Write your answer below:

A B C D E F G H I J K L M N O P Q R S T U V W X Y Z

MB is to OC as LZ is to ___?

Answer:

14) Select the pair of words, one from each group that are most opposite in meaning to each other from the options given below. Write your answer below:

(Hear Nice Shout) (Find Loud Whisper)

A. Shout Whisper
B. Hear Loud
C. Shout Loud
D. Nice Find
E. Hear Whisper

Answer:

15) Choose the correct answer by completing the following functions and sums with the correct numbers and signs as appropriate. Write your answer below:

45 − 9 ÷ 3 x ___ = 13 + 26

A. 5
B. 4
C. 3
D. 2
E. 1

Answer:

16) Choose the correct answer for the following problem. Write your answer below:

When 6 is subtracted from a number, it gives an answer which is 7 more than 33. What is the number?

A. 39
B. 40
C. 42
D. 44
E. 46

Answer:

17) The words in brackets are formed from the main word. Identify the pattern to work out the missing word from the options given. Write your answer below:

Minnow (won), swap (___), cannot (ton)

A. PAW
B. LAW
C. RAW
D. WAP
E. ABC

Answer:

18) Three consecutive letters are removed from the word in CAPITALS. These letters make a word. From the options, find the missing letters to complete the sentence. Write your answer below:

The vase was available in lots of different SHS.

A. APE
B. ARE
C. EAR
D. AND
E. EAT

Answer:

19) A four letter word is hidden between two words in the sentence below. These two words are always next to each other, but there may be punctuation between them. Find this four letter word from one of the options. Write your answer below:

To make the charger stronger on the outside, nylon was used as it is less resistant to breaking.

A. make the
B. used as
C. stronger on
D. resistant to
E. outside nylon

Answer:

20) A four letter word is hidden between two words in the sentence below. These two words are always next to each other, but there may be punctuation between them. Find this four letter word from one of the options. Write your answer below:

One must take precautions in the event of a tornado especially if it is high on the F-scale.

A. tornado especially
B. take precautions
C. especially if
D. high on
E. must take

Answer:

Verbal Reasoning - Test 26

21) Find the number that best complete the series. Fill in the missing blank with one of the following options and write your answer below:

891 spades, 297 forks, 99 spades, ___, 11 spades

A. 81 forks
B. 33 forks
C. 55 spades
D. 66 forks
E. 76 forks

Answer:

22) Three consecutive letters have been taken out of a word. Select which three letters have been omitted from the options. Write your answer below:

The young adventurer was due to EM___K on his most dangerous journey yet.

A. BIT
B. BAT
C. BAR
D. CAR
E. EAR

Answer:

23) Write the letter that will complete the word in front of the brackets and begin the word after the brackets. The SAME letter must fit into BOTH sets of brackets. Write your answer below:

mis (_) ong, mas (_) ick

Answer:

24) Select the two words inside the brackets that are connected in some way to the words outside the brackets. Write your answer below:

Riddha only likes certain types of animals. She likes the WOLF TIGER (cow, rabbit, fox, sheep, lion)

Answer:

25) Find one word from each group that together makes one correctly spelt word. The letters must not be rearranged. The word from the first group must always be used first. Write your answer below:

The building of the bridge went like (clock, watch, time) (job, office, work).

A. Timejob
B. Clockwork
C. Watchwork
D. Clockjob
E. Timeoffice

Answer:

26) Find the pair of letters that will continue the series. The alphabet is provided below to help you. Write your answer below:

A B C D E F G H I J K L M N O P Q R S T U V W X Y Z

11DR, 22CS, 33BT, 33AU, 44ZV, 55 ___?

Answer:

27) Select the TWO odd words from the options given. Write your answer below:

Candle, mirror, moon, lamp, torch

A. Mirror moon
B. Lamp torch
C. Candle mirror
D. Candle moon
E. Mirror torch

Answer:

28) Choose the correct answer by completing the following functions and sums with the correct numbers and signs as appropriate. Write your answer below:

52 − ___ × 2 = 48 ÷ 3 − 4

A. 14
B. 20
C. 15
D. 25
E. 19

Answer:

29) Choose the correct answer for the following problem. Write your answer below:

A cake costs 55p more than a packet of croissants. Together they cost £3.15. How much is a pack of croissants?

A. £1.10
B. £1.15
C. £1.20
D. £1.25
E. £1.30

Answer:

30) Read the information provided and choose the single best answer for the question. Write your answer below:

A certain month has 5 Wednesdays and the 5th of the month is a Saturday. What date is the third Wednesday of the month?

A. 14th
B. 15th
C. 16th
D. 17th
E. 18th

Answer:

Verbal Reasoning - Test 26

31) Three consecutive letters are removed from the word in CAPITALS. These letters make a word. From the options, find the missing letters to complete the sentence. Write your answer below:

Jack waited to be INMED of the judge's decision.

A. FUR
B. FAT
C. FAR
D. FOR
E. FIT

Answer:

32) Find the number that best complete the series. Fill in the missing blank with one of the following options and write your answer below:

96, 48, 24, ___ , 6

A. 18
B. 12
C. 20
D. 8
E. 10

Answer:

33) Select the word from the brackets that will complete the sentence in the most sensible way. Write your answer below:

Monday is to DAY as November is to (date, year, month)

Answer:

34) Find one word from each group that together makes one correctly spelt word. The letters must not be rearranged. The word from the first group must always be used first. Write your answer below:

The (mug, glass, cup) (tray, board, shelf) contained a number of plates and bowls.

A. Glassshelf   D. Cuptray
B. Mugtray   E. Mugboard
C. Cupboard

Answer:

35) Find the pair of letters that will continue the series. The alphabet is provided below to help you. Write your answer below:

A B C D E F G H I J K L M N O P Q R S T U V W X Y Z

HM, KP, NS, QV, TY, ___?

Answer:

36) Find the pair of letters that will complete the sentence in the best way. The alphabet is provided below to help you. Write your answer below:

A B C D E F G H I J K L M N O P Q R S T U V W X Y Z

KC is to ME as SL is to ___?

Answer:

37) Select the pair of words, one from each group that are most opposite in meaning to each other from the options given. Write your answer below:

(When Food Hot) (Eat Which Cold)

A. Hot Cold
B. Food Eat
C. When Which
D. Food Cold
E. When Eat

Answer:

38) Select the TWO odd words from the options given. Write your answer below:

Unhappy, tired, dreary, sad, content

A. Tired content
B. Unhappy content
C. Dreary sad
D. Sad tired
E. Unhappy dreary

Answer:

39) Select the two words inside the brackets that are connected in some way to the words outside the brackets. Write your answer below:

SWIM RUN (jog, sit, row, bus, car)

Answer:

40) Select the word from the brackets that will complete the sentence in the most sensible way. Write your answer below:

Bee is to HONEY as cow is to (milk, grass, farm)

Answer:

Verbal Reasoning - Test 27

Time allowed for this paper : 60 minutes

Instructions for Best Practice:

> Attempt all of the questions.
> Ensure that your answers are clearly marked in the answer boxes.
> Calculators and rulers must not be used.
> Equipment recommended: 2 x Pencil & 1 x Eraser.

Verbal Reasoning - Test 27

1) Three consecutive letters have been taken out of a word. Select which three letters have been omitted from the options. Write your answer below:

   F___

   A. OAR
   B. USE
   C. ARK
   D. ONE
   E. OAT

   Answer:

2) You are required to move one letter from the first word to the second word, creating **two new words**. Write your answer below:

   HEART DEER.

   Answer:

3) Using the provided code, complete the following sums writing your answer in <u>letters</u>:

   a = 1, b = 4, c = 9, d = 6, e = 2

   Solve: c − d − e = ___?

   Answer:

4) Using the provided code, complete the following sums writing your answer in <u>letters</u>:

   a = 1, b = 4, c = 9, d = 6, e = 2

   Solve: d x e − c + a = ___?

   Answer:

5) Select the word from the brackets that will **complete the sentence in the most sensible way**. Write your answer below:

   Money is to BANK as bread is to (bakery, food, eat)

   Answer:

6) Find one word from **each group** that together makes **one correctly spelt word**. The letters must not be rearranged. The word from the first group **must always be used first**. Write your answer below:

   The (mumble, mutter, bumble) (bee, fly, wasp) should not be able to fly, yet it continues to do so.

   A. Mumblebee   D. Bumblefly
   B. Mutterwasp   E. Mutterfly
   C. Bumblebee

   Answer:

7) **Find the pair of letters** that will complete the sentence in the best way. The alphabet is provided below to help you. Write your answer below:

   A B C D E F G H I J K L M N O P Q R S T U V W X Y Z

   NO is to RS as WX is to ___?

   Answer:

8) Select the pair of words, one from each group that are most opposite in meaning to each other from the options given below. Write your answer below:

   The opposite of (Deer Date Dusk) is (Day Dear Dawn).

   A. Deer Day
   B. Dusk Day
   C. Date Dear
   D. Deer Date
   E. Dusk Dawn

   Answer:

9) Choose the correct answer by **completing the following functions and sums with the correct numbers and signs** as appropriate. Write your answer below:

   7 + 8 = ___ + 5

   A. 8
   B. 9
   C. 10
   D. 11
   E. 12

   Answer:

10) Choose the correct answer for the following problem. Write your answer below:

    50% of a number multiplied by 5 is equal to four less than 49? What is the number?

    A. 14
    B. 16
    C. 18
    D. 20
    E. 22

    Answer:

Verbal Reasoning

Verbal Reasoning - Test 27

11) Three consecutive letters are removed from the word in CAPITALS. These letters make a word. From the options, find the missing letters to complete the sentence. Write your answer below:

The police asked the witness to DESCE the incident.

A. RIB
B. RUN
C. RUT
D. BIB
E. BUN

Answer:

12) In each set of numbers, the number in the brackets is related to the two numbers either side of it. Find this relation to work out the missing number '(?)' in the third set. Choose one of the options and write your answer below:

5 (25) 5, 6 (42) 7, 9 (?) 2

A. 13   D. 18
B. 23   E. 21
C. 12

Answer:

13) In each set of numbers, the number in the brackets is related to the two numbers either side of it. Find this relation to work out the missing number '(?)' in the third set. Choose one of the option and write your answer below:

11 (44) 4, 13 (65) 5, 18 (?) 3

A. 54   D. 29
B. 15   E. 36
C. 5

Answer:

14) Find the pair of letters that will complete the sentence in the best way. The alphabet is provided below to help you. Write your answer below:

A B C D E F G H I J K L M N O P Q R S T U V W X Y Z

IK is to JJ as JL is to __?

Answer:

15) Select the pair of words, one from each group that are most opposite in meaning to each other from the options given. Write your answer below:

(Arrive Fall Descent) (Crave Loose Ascent)

A. Descent Ascent
B. Fall Ascent
C. Loose Arrive
D. Loose Fall
E. Fall Crave

Answer:

16) Select the TWO odd words from the options given. Write your answer below:

Daffodil, daisy, rose, garden, oak

A. Rose garden
B. Daisy daffodil
C. Daffodil oak
D. Garden oak
E. Garden daisy

Answer:

17) Write the letter that will complete the word in front of the brackets and begin the word after the brackets. The SAME letter must fit into BOTH sets of brackets. Write your answer below:

mis (_) rip, mas (_) ick

Answer:

18) Select the two words inside the brackets that are connected in some way to the words outside the brackets. Write your answer below:

Jenny only likes certain types of animals. She likes the RABBIT, HAMSTER (cat, bear, cow, dog, sheep)

Answer:

19) Three consecutive letters have been taken out of a word. Select which three letters have been omitted from the options. Write your answer below:

HU___E

A. MAN
B. MAT
C. MET
D. MEN
E. CAT

Answer:

20) You are required to move one letter from the first word to the second word, creating two new words. Write your answer below:

HERD RAFT
_____ _____ was of an outstanding quality for someone her age.

Answer:

Verbal Reasoning - Test 27

21) Work out the relationship between the word and the code to solve the code and write your answer below:

A B C D E F G H I J K L M N O P Q R S T U V W X Y Z

TENNIS is to VCPLKQ. <u>Decode</u> the following: NYEPQQUC.

Answer:

22) Work out the relationship between the word and the code to solve the code and write your answer below:

A B C D E F G H I J K L M N O P Q R S T U V W X Y Z

TENNIS is to VCPLKQ. <u>Decode</u> the following: TSIZA.

Answer:

23) Write the letter that will complete the word in front of the brackets and begin the word after the brackets. The SAME letter must fit into BOTH sets of brackets. Write your answer below:

mot (_) and, suc (_) ack

Answer:

24) Select the two words inside the brackets that are connected in some way to the words outside the brackets. Write your answer below:

CAR BUS (helicopter, lorry, van, train, plane)

Answer:

25) Find one word from each group that together makes one correctly spelt word. The letters must not be rearranged. The word from the first group must always be used first. Write your answer below:

How beautiful a (cheese, yoghurt, butter) (lizard, spider, fly) is in the springtime!

A. Butterfly
B. Cheesespider
C. Butterlizard
D. Yoghurtfly
E. Cheeselizard

Answer:

26) Find the pair of letters that will continue the series. The alphabet is provided below to help you. Write your answer below:

A B C D E F G H I J K L M N O P Q R S T U V W X Y Z

BP, XL, TH, PD, LZ, ___?

Answer:

27) Choose the correct answer for the following problem. Write your answer below:

Three hundred and sixty divided by ten is equivalent to nine multiplied by one third of a number. What is the number?

A. 15
B. 12
C. 21
D. 24
E. 27

Answer:

28) Read the information provided and choose the single best answer for the question. Write your answer below:

Sanjay, Simran, Danny and Abigail are four teenagers. Sanjay and Simran are the only ones who like both orange and mango juice. Simran and Abigail are the only ones who like both mango and lychee juice. Danny and Sanjay are the only ones who like both passionfruit and apple juice.

Who likes mango and orange juice but not passionfruit juice?

A. Sanjay   D. Abigail
B. Simran   E. None
C. Danny

Answer:

29) Read the information provided and choose the single best answer for the question. Write your answer below:

Sanjay, Simran, Danny and Abigail are four teenagers. Sanjay and Simran are the only ones who like both orange and mango juice. Simran and Abigail are the only ones who like both mango and lychee juice. Danny and Sanjay are the only ones who like both passionfruit and apple juice.

What is the only juice that Sanjay doesn't like?

A. Orange   D. Passionfruit
B. Mango   E. Apple
C. Lychee

Answer:

30) The words in brackets are formed from the main word. Identify the pattern to work out the missing word from the options given. Write your answer below:

Nutmeg (gem), relieve (eve), beware (?)

A. ERA
B. WAR
C. ARE
D. WEB
E. BAR

Answer:

Verbal Reasoning - Test 27

31) A four letter word is hidden between two words in the sentence below. These two words are always next to each other, but there may be punctuation between them. Find this four letter word from one of the options. Write your answer below:

Robert will get his brown belt in judo next Wednesday.

A. Robert will
B. belt in
C. his brown
D. judo next
E. next wednesday

Answer:

32) A four letter word is hidden between two words in the sentence below. These two words are always next to each other, but there may be punctuation between them. Find this four letter word from one of the options. Write your answer below:

You must wash the jacket of your tuxedo separately.

A. tuxedo separately
B. wash the
C. jacket of
D. your tuxedo
E. must wash

Answer:

33) Find the number that best complete the series. Fill in the missing blank with one of the following options and write your answer below:

88, 84, 44, 42, __ , 21

A. 28
B. 24
C. 36
D. 22
E. 37

Answer:

34) Select the word from the brackets that will complete the sentence in the most sensible way. Write your answer below:

Swim is to POOL as Basketball is to (court, field, pitch)

Answer:

35) Find the pair of letters that will continue the series. The alphabet is provided below to help you. Write your answer below:

A B C D E F G H I J K L M N O P Q R S T U V W X Y Z

GT, HS, IR, JQ, KP, __?

Answer:

36) Select the TWO odd words from the options given. Write your answer below:

Socks, sandals, boots, trainers, feet

A. Socks sandals
B. Socks feet
C. Boots trainers
D. Sandals feet
E. Sandals trainers

Answer:

37) Choose the correct answer by completing the following functions and sums with the correct numbers and signs as appropriate. Write your answer below:

__ × 6 ÷ 3 + 2 = 12 × (1 + 6 ÷ 3 + 2)

A. 14
B. 33
C. 29
D. 26
E. 17

Answer:

38) The words in brackets are formed from the main word. Identify the pattern to work out the missing word from the options given. Write your answer below:

Declare (era), pyramid (dim), agendas (?)

A. ANE
B. DEN
C. SAD
D. DAG
E. AND

Answer:

39) Three consecutive letters are removed from the word in CAPITALS. These letters make a word. From the options, find the missing letters to complete the sentence. Write your answer below:

Will MED his position on the map.

A. ACE
B. ARC
C. ARK
D. ARM
E. ACT

Answer:

40) Find the number that best complete the series. Fill in the missing blank with one of the following options and write your answer below:

585, 90, 195, 60, __ , 30

A. 45
B. 50
C. 55
D. 65
E. 70

Answer:

Verbal Reasoning - Test 28

Time allowed for this paper : 60 minutes

Instructions for Best Practice:

> Attempt all of the questions.
> Ensure that your answers are clearly marked in the answer boxes.
> Calculators and rulers must not be used.
> Equipment recommended: 2 x Pencil & 1 x Eraser.

Verbal Reasoning - Test 28

Marks

1) Work out the relationship between the word and the code to solve the code and write your answer below:

   A B C D E F G H I J K L M N O P Q R S T U V W X Y Z

   FINGER is to ILQJHU. What is the code for TOE?

   Answer:

2) Work out the relationship between the word and the code to solve the code and write your answer below:

   A B C D E F G H I J K L M N O P Q R S T U V W X Y Z

   FINGER is to ILQJHU. What is the code for HAND?

   Answer:

3) Using the provided code, complete the following sums writing your answer in <u>letters</u>:

   a = 1, b = 4, c = 9, d = 6, e = 2

   Solve: b ÷ e − a = ___?

   Answer:

4) Select the word from the brackets that will complete the sentence in the most sensible way. Write your answer below:

   North is to SOUTH as east is to (west, compass, pole)

   Answer:

5) Find one word from each group that together makes one correctly spelt word. The letters must not be rearranged. The word from the first group must always be used first. Write your answer below:

   The (butter, milk, cheese) (mug, urn, cup) was found in the middle of the garden.

   A. Buttercup   D. Milkurn
   B. Milkmug   E. Buttermug
   C. Cheesecup

   Answer:

6) Select the TWO odd words from the options given. Write your answer below:

   Happiness, sadness, frown, envy, cry, anxiousness

   A. Frown sadness
   B. Happiness cry
   C. Envy sadness
   D. Envy cry
   E. Frown cry

   Answer:

7) Choose the correct answer by completing the following functions and sums with the correct numbers and signs as appropriate. Write your answer below:

   (26 × ___) ÷ 13 = 128 − 124

   A. 13
   B. 6
   C. 5
   D. 2
   E. 8

   Answer:

8) The words in brackets are formed from the main word. Identify the pattern to work out the missing word from the options given. Write your answer below:

   Straw (war), crab (bar), backstab (?)

   A. TAB
   B. SAB
   C. CAS
   D. SAT
   E. BAT

   Answer:

9) Three consecutive letters are removed from the word in CAPITALS. These letters make a word. From the options, find the missing letters to complete the sentence. Write your answer below:

   Ben was left in DESP by the accident.

   A. ART
   B. ARM
   C. AIR
   D. BAR
   E. ACT

   Answer:

10) Find one word from each group that together makes one correctly spelt word. The letters must not be rearranged. The word from the first group must always be used first. Write your answer below:

    (racket, ball, bat) (house, room, garden)

    A. Rackethouse
    B. Ballroom
    C. Bathouse
    D. Ballgarden
    E. Batgarden

    Answer:

Verbal Reasoning - Test 28

11) Find the pair of letters that will continue the series. The alphabet is provided below to help you. Write your answer below:

A B C D E F G H I J K L M N O P Q R S T U V W X Y Z

EO, CQ, AS, YU, WW, ___?

Answer:

12) Choose the correct answer for the following problem. Write your answer below:

What number is one-quarter of 76?

A. 19
B. 18
C. 17
D. 16
E. 15

Answer:

13) Read the information provided and choose the single best answer for the question. Write your answer below:

Ariana, Brian, Callum, Dinesh and Esha all work in the same office. Callum arrived on time. Esha arrived after Callum but before Dinesh. Brian arrived early and Ariana was the last to arrive.

How many people arrived after Brian?

A. 1   D. 4
B. 2   E. 5
C. 3

Answer:

14) Read the information provided and choose the single best answer for the question. Write your answer below:

Ariana, Brian, Callum, Dinesh and Esha all work in the same office. Callum arrived on time. Esha arrived after Callum but before Dinesh. Brian arrived early and Ariana was the last to arrive.

How many people arrived before Esha?

A. 1   D. 4
B. 2   E. 5
C. 3

Answer:

15) The words in brackets are formed from the main word. Identify the pattern to work out the missing word from the options given. Write your answer below:

Stew (wet), snow (won), forfeit (?)

A. TIE
B. ROT
C. FOR
D. FIT
E. TOR

Answer:

16) A four letter word is hidden between two words in the sentence below. These two words are always next to each other, but there may be punctuation between them. Find this four letter word from one of the options. Write your answer below:

I love to set up my stall by the sea, selling lemonade to raise money for charity.

A. my stall
B. selling lemonade
C. love to
D. raise money
E. lemonade to

Answer:

17) A four letter word is hidden between two words in the sentence below. These two words are always next to each other, but there may be punctuation between them. Find this four letter word from one of the options. Write your answer below:

In Britain, afternoon tea still holds value.

A. In Britain
B. tea still
C. still holds
D. afternoon tea
E. holds value

Answer:

18) Find the number that best complete the series. Fill in the missing blank with one of the following options and write your answer below:

3, 30, 6, ___ , 9, 24

A. 12
B. 15
C. 25
D. 18
E. 27

Answer:

19) Choose the correct answer for the following problem. Write your answer below:

Harry buys 2 chocolate bars and a packet of crisps for £2.50. 1 chocolate bar and 1 packet of crisps costs £1.80. How much is a packet of crisps?

A. £1.00
B. £1.10
C. £1.15
D. £1.25
E. £1.20

Answer:

20) Three consecutive letters are removed from the word in CAPITALS. These letters make a word. From the options, find the missing letters to complete the sentence. Write your answer below:

The Joker was a MEN to Batman.

A. ANT
B. ARK
C. ART
D. ATE
E. ACE

Answer:

Verbal Reasoning - Test 28

21) In each set of numbers, the number in the brackets is related to the two numbers either side of it. Find this relation to work out the missing number '(?)' in the third set. Choose one of the options and write your answer below:

2 (18) 9, 4 (28) 7, 6 (?) 6

A. 18   D. 6
B. 15   E. 36
C. 51

Answer:

22) In each set of numbers, the number in the brackets is related to the two numbers either side of it. Find this relation to work out the missing number '(?)' in the third set. Choose one of the option and write your answer below:

3 (21) 7, 3 (33) 11, 3 (?) 14

A. 7   D. 42
B. 11   E. 16
C. 9

Answer:

23) Using the provided code, complete the following sums writing your answer in <u>letters</u>:

a = 5, b = 10, c = 4, d = 2, e = 8

Solve: b ÷ a = ___?

Answer:

24) Write the letter that will **complete the word in front of the brackets** and **begin the word after the brackets**. The SAME letter must fit into BOTH sets of brackets. Write your answer below:

sca (_) ilk, pal (_) ast

Answer:

25) Three consecutive letters have been taken out of a word. Select which three letters have been omitted from the options. Write your answer below:

The ___LE for my phone charger snapped.

A. CAR
B. CAT
C. BAR
D. DAB
E. CAB

Answer:

26) You are required to move one letter from the first word to the second word, creating **two new words**. Write your answer below:

GREED BEAN.

Answer:

27) Select the two words **inside the brackets** that are connected in some way to the words **outside the brackets**. Write your answer below:

WASP ANT (robin, rabbit, beetle, rat, cockroach)

Answer:

28) Select the word from the brackets that will **complete the sentence in the most sensible way**. Write your answer below:

Grasshopper is to INSECT as robin is to (bird, red, fly)

Answer:

29) Find the **pair of letters** that will continue the series. The alphabet is provided below to help you. Write your answer below:

A B C D E F G H I J K L M N O P Q R S T U V W X Y Z

PP, ON, NL, MJ, LH, ___?

Answer:

30) Select the pair of words, one from each group that are most opposite in meaning to each other from the options given. Write your answer below:

The opposite of (Try Fill Laugh) is (Cry Imagine Dodge).

A. Laugh Cry
B. Try Cry
C. Laugh Imagine
D. Try Dodge
E. Fill Imagine

Answer:

Verbal Reasoning - Test 28

31) Select the TWO odd words from the options given. Write your answer below:

Fish, steam, vegetables, fry, roast

A. Fish steam
B. Fry roast
C. Fish vegetables
D. Vegetables steam
E. Fry fish

Answer:

32) Choose the correct answer by **completing the following functions and sums** with the **correct numbers and signs** as appropriate. Write your answer below:

84 ÷ (14 − 7) = 144 ÷ ___

A. 12
B. 8
C. 14
D. 2
E. 16

Answer:

33) Find the number that best complete the series. Fill in the **missing blank** with one of the following options and write your answer below:

___ , 48, 8, 44, 12, 40

A. 60
B. 1
C. 8
D. 52
E. 4

Answer:

34) Three consecutive letters have been taken out of a word. Select which three letters **have been omitted** from the options. Write your answer below:

The ES___E was not easy and required a lot of preparation.

A. COP
B. CAP
C. CAN
D. COD
E. COT

Answer:

35) You are required to move one letter from the first word to the second word, creating **two new words**. Write your answer below:

TOY READ.

Answer:

36) Write the letter that will **complete the word in front of the brackets** and **begin the word after the brackets**. The SAME letter must fit into BOTH sets of brackets. Write your answer below:

cal (_) eet, lea (_) ire

Answer:

37) Select the two words **inside the brackets** that are connected in some way to the words **outside the brackets**. Write your answer below:

SWEETCORN PEAS (pineapple, plums, carrots, broccoli, grapes)

Answer:

38) Find the pair of letters that will complete the sentence in the best way. The alphabet is provided below to help you. Write your answer below:

A B C D E F G H I J K L M N O P Q R S T U V W X Y Z

DL is to FK as MS is to ___?

Answer:

39) Find the pair of letters that will complete the sentence in the best way. The alphabet is provided below to help you. Write your answer below:

A B C D E F G H I J K L M N O P Q R S T U V W X Y Z

PA is to MC as TF is to ___?

Answer:

40) Select the pair of words, one from each group that are most opposite in meaning to each other from the options given below. Write your answer below:

The opposite of (Leave Close Up) is (Shut Fall Down).

A. Up Down
B. Leave Shut
C. Close Shut
D. Up Shut
E. Close Down

Answer:

Verbal Reasoning - Test 29

Time allowed for this paper : 60 minutes

Instructions for Best Practice:

> Attempt all of the questions.
> Ensure that your answers are clearly marked in the answer boxes.
> Calculators and rulers must not be used.
> Equipment recommended: 2 x Pencil & 1 x Eraser.

Verbal Reasoning - Test 29

1) Three consecutive letters have been taken out of a word. Select which three letters have been omitted from the options. Write your answer below:

   My favourite past paper is that of verbal REA___ING.

   A. SAT
   B. SIT
   C. SON
   D. SUN
   E. SAW

   Answer:

2) You are required to move one letter from the first word to the second word, creating two new words. Write your answer below:

   CANE UNIT

   'Only you ____ _____ the two sides of the country!' shouted the patriotic politician.

   Answer:

3) Work out the relationship between the word and the code to solve the code and write your answer below:

   A B C D E F G H I J K L M N O P Q R S T U V W X Y Z

   FINGER is to ILQJHU. What is the code for FACE?

   Answer:

4) Work out the relationship between the word and the code to solve the code and write your answer below:

   A B C D E F G H I J K L M N O P Q R S T U V W X Y Z

   FINGER is to ILQJHU. Decode the following: HDU?

   Answer:

5) Using the provided code, complete the following sums writing your answer in letters:

   a = 5, b = 10, c = 4, d = 2, e = 8

   Solve: c x d = __?

   Answer:

6) Using the provided code, complete the following sums writing your answer in letters:

   a = 5, b = 10, c = 4, d = 2, e = 8

   Solve: c ÷ d + e = __?

   Answer:

7) Find one word from each group that together makes one correctly spelt word. The letters must not be rearranged. The word from the first group must always be used first. Write your answer below:

   The most refreshing drink is a (butter, milk, cheese) (stir, still, shake).

   A. Butterstir   D. Cheesestill
   B. Milkshake   E. Milkstir
   C. Buttershake

   Answer:

8) Find the pair of letters that will continue the series. The alphabet is provided below to help you. Write your answer below:

   A B C D E F G H I J K L M N O P Q R S T U V W X Y Z

   KP, LN, ML, NJ, OH, __?

   Answer:

9) Select the pair of words, one from each group that are most opposite in meaning to each other from the options given. Write your answer below:

   (Enter Tall Bus) (Climb Leave Tree)

   A. Enter Climb
   B. Tree Bus
   C. Tall Leave
   D. Enter Leave
   E. Bus Leave

   Answer:

10) Select the TWO odd words from the options given. Write your answer below:

    Sister, friend, companion, comrade, brother.

    A. Friend companion
    B. Comrade brother
    C. Sister friend
    D. Companion comrade
    E. Brother sister

    Answer:

Verbal Reasoning - Test 29

Marks

11) Choose the correct answer by **completing the following functions and sums** with the **correct numbers and signs** as appropriate. Write your answer below:

51 + ___ ÷ 4 = 3 × 18

A. 4
B. 8
C. 12
D. 16
E. 18

Answer:

12) Choose the correct answer **for the following problem**. Write your answer below:

What number is three-fifths of 75?

A. 30   D. 45
B. 35   E. 50
C. 40

Answer:

13) The words in brackets are formed from the main word. Identify the **pattern** to work out the **missing word** from the options given. Write your answer below:

Angel (leg), turnip (pin), kidnap (?)

A. NID
B. PIK
C. PID
D. AND
E. PAN

Answer:

14) Three consecutive letters are removed from the word in CAPITALS. These letters make a word. From the options, **find the missing letters** to complete the sentence. Write your answer below:

The BARDER was working the evening shift at the bar.

A. ONE
B. TWO
C. SIX
D. TEN
E. SIT

Answer:

15) In each set of numbers, the number in the brackets is related to **the two numbers either side of it**. Find this relation to work out the missing number '(?)' in the third set. Choose one of the options and write your answer below:

13 (26) 2, 11 (121) 11, 8 (?) 9

A. 17   D. 28
B. 10   E. 72
C. 36

Answer:

16) In each set of numbers, the number in the brackets is related to **the two numbers either side of it**. Find this relation to work out the missing number '(?)' in the third set. Choose one of the option and write your answer below:

4 (64) 16, 7 (14) 2, 14 (?) 3

A. 8
B. 17
C. 42
D. 28
E. 4

Answer:

17) Find the number that best complete the series. Fill in the **missing blank** with one of the following options and write your answer below:

___ , 70, 21, 63, 28, 56, 35

A. 97
B. 84
C. 7
D. 14
E. 77

Answer:

18) The words in brackets are formed from the main word. Identify the **pattern** to work out the **missing word** from the options given. Write your answer below:

Bathtub (but), compare (era), symbol (?)

A. BYS
B. MOL
C. MYL
D. LOB
E. SOM

Answer:

19) Select the two words **inside the brackets** that are connected in some way to the words **outside the brackets**. Write your answer below:

Ali's favourite planets are EARTH, MARS, (Venus, moon, Sun, Saturn, star)

Answer:

20) Select the word from the brackets that will **complete the sentence** in the most sensible way. Write your answer below:

Multiple is to DIVIDE as add is to (number, subtract, maths, seven, eight)

Answer:

Verbal Reasoning - Test 29

21) Three consecutive letters have been taken out of a word. Select which three letters have been omitted from the options. Write your answer below:

REH___SE

A. EAR
B. EAT
C. ATE
D. BAR
E. CAR

Answer:

22) You are required to move one letter from the first word to the second word, creating two new words. Write your answer below:

HORSE CAT.

Answer:

23) Write the letter that will complete the word in front of the brackets and begin the word after the brackets. The SAME letter must fit into BOTH sets of brackets. Write your answer below:

cal (_) eat, tea (_) oat

Answer:

24) Select the word from the brackets that will complete the sentence in the most sensible way. Write your answer below:

Rain is to UMBRELLA as sun is to (sunglasses, hot, sky, moon, sun)

Answer:

25) Find one word from each group that together makes one correctly spelt word. The letters must not be rearranged. The word from the first group must always be used first. Write your answer below:

(sun, moon, star) (set, stay, leave)

A. Moonleave
B. Starset
C. Sunleave
D. Moonstay
E. Sunset

Answer:

26) Find the pair of letters that will continue the series. The alphabet is provided below to help you. Write your answer below:

A B C D E F G H I J K L M N O P Q R S T U V W X Y Z

BD, DC, BB, DA, BZ, ___?

Answer:

27) Select the pair of words, one from each group that are most opposite in meaning to each other from the options given below. Write your answer below:

(East Leave How) (Join West Now)

A. Leave Now
B. How Now
C. Join West
D. East Now
E. East West

Answer:

28) Select the TWO odd words from the options given. Write your answer below:

Create, destroy, break, build, make, form, construct

A. Destroy break
B. Build create
C. Create destroy
D. Build make
E. Make break

Answer:

29) Choose the correct answer by completing the following functions and sums with the correct numbers and signs as appropriate. Write your answer below:

156 − 24 = 11 × ___ ÷ (2 × 3)

A. 54
B. 60
C. 72
D. 76
E. 84

Answer:

30) Choose the correct answer for the following problem. Write your answer below:

Liz has three times as much money as Carl. Carl has 70p less than £3.00. How much money does Liz have?

A. £6.50
B. £6.60
C. £6.70
D. £6.80
E. £6.90

Answer:

Verbal Reasoning - Test 29

31) Read the information provided and choose the single best answer for the question. Write your answer below:

A month has 4 Thursdays in it and the second Tuesday of that month is the 11th.

What date is the final Friday of that month?

A. 27th
B. 28th
C. 29th
D. 30th
E. 31st

Answer:

32) Read the information provided and choose the single best answer for the question. Write your answer below:

A month has 4 Thursdays in it and the second Tuesday of that month is the 11th.

What date is the first Monday of that month?

A. 1st
B. 2nd
C. 3rd
D. 4th
E. 5th

Answer:

33) A four letter word is hidden between two words in the sentence below. These two words are always next to each other, but there may be punctuation between them. Find this four letter word from one of the options. Write your answer below:

This area charms us with scenic mountain peaks and several flowing waterfalls.

A. area charms
B. mountain peaks
C. flowing waterfalls
D. and several
E. with scenic

Answer:

34) A four letter word is hidden between two words in the sentence below. These two words are always next to each other, but there may be punctuation between them. Find this four letter word from one of the options. Write your answer below:

He accidentally released the balloon, and it flew high into the sky beyond his reach.

A. high into
B. accidentally released
C. sky beyond
D. his reach
E. the balloon

Answer:

35) Find the number that best complete the series. Fill in the missing blank with one of the following options and write your answer below:

15, 45, __ , 40, 25, 35, 30

A. 20
B. 25
C. 30
D. 35
E. 40

Answer:

36) Write the letter that will complete the word in front of the brackets and begin the word after the brackets. The SAME letter must fit into BOTH sets of brackets. Write your answer below:

lea (_) ear, hea (_) art

Answer:

37) Select the two words inside the brackets that are connected in some way to the words outside the brackets. Write your answer below:

STATION SCHOOL (hospital, park, beach, bank, road, pavement, river)

Answer:

38) Find the pair of letters that will complete the sentence in the best way. The alphabet is provided below to help you. Write your answer below:

A B C D E F G H I J K L M N O P Q R S T U V W X Y Z

JS is to KR as FN is to ___?

Answer:

39) Three consecutive letters are removed from the word in CAPITALS. These letters make a word. From the options, find the missing letters to complete the sentence. Write your answer below:

Dean was cast as the lead CHARER in the school play.

A. ARC
B. ARK
C. ART
D. ACT
E. ANT

Answer:

40) Find the pair of letters that will complete the sentence in the best way. The alphabet is provided below to help you. Write your answer below:

A B C D E F G H I J K L M N O P Q R S T U V W X Y Z

WN is to UP as ND is to ___?

Answer:

Verbal Reasoning - Test 30

Time allowed for this paper : 60 minutes

Instructions for Best Practice:

> Attempt all of the questions.
> Ensure that your answers are clearly marked in the answer boxes.
> Calculators and rulers must not be used.
> Equipment recommended: 2 x Pencil & 1 x Eraser.

Verbal Reasoning - Test 30

1) Work out the relationship between the word and the code to solve the code and write your answer below:

   A B C D E F G H I J K L M N O P Q R S T U V W X Y Z

   FINGER is to ILQJHU. <u>Decode</u> the following: IRRW.

   Answer:

2) Work out the relationship between the word and the code to solve the code and write your answer below:

   A B C D E F G H I J K L M N O P Q R S T U V W X Y Z

   FINGER is to ILQJHU. <u>Decode</u> the following: WKXPE.

   Answer:

3) Using the provided code, complete the following sums writing your answer in <u>letters</u>:

   a = 5, b = 10, c = 4, d = 2, e = 8

   Solve: b ÷ a × d = ___?

   Answer:

4) Using the provided code, complete the following sums writing your answer in <u>letters</u>:

   a = 5, b = 10, c = 4, d = 2, e = 8

   Solve: a × d − b + c = ___?

   Answer:

5) Find one word from each group that together makes one correctly spelt word. The letters must not be rearranged. The word from the first group must always be used first. Write your answer below:

   He effortlessly ate his dinner using his (ham, steak, chop) (sticks, skewers, twigs).

   A. Hamsticks
   B. Steakskewers
   C. Chopsticks
   D. Hamtwigs
   E. Chopskewers

   Answer:

6) Find the pair of letters that will continue the series. The alphabet is provided below to help you. Write your answer below:

   A B C D E F G H I J K L M N O P Q R S T U V W X Y Z

   DJ, EL, FN, GP, HR ___?

   Answer:

7) Select the TWO odd words from the options given. Write your answer below:

   Oak, gold, acrylic, copper, iron, tin, silver

   A. Gold copper
   B. Oak acrylic
   C. Copper oak
   D. Iron gold
   E. Acrylic copper

   Answer:

8) Choose the correct answer by completing the following functions and sums with the correct numbers and signs as appropriate. Write your answer below:

   24 × (6 + 4 − ___) = 11 × 11 − 1

   A. 5
   B. 6
   C. 7
   D. 3
   E. 4

   Answer:

9) The words in brackets are formed from the main word. Identify the pattern to work out the missing word from the options given. Write your answer below:

   Kneecaps (spa), minnow (won), armpit (?)

   A. PIT
   B. RAM
   C. PAR
   D. RAT
   E. TIP

   Answer:

10) Three consecutive letters are removed from the word in CAPITALS. These letters make a word. From the options, find the missing letters to complete the sentence. Write your answer below:

    Claire wanted to know the REAING behind her colleague's decision.

    A. SUN
    B. SON
    C. SAT
    D. SIT
    E. SUM

    Answer:

Verbal Reasoning

Verbal Reasoning - Test 30

11) In each set of numbers, the number in the brackets is related to the two numbers either side of it. Find this relation to work out the missing number '(?)' in the third set. Choose one of the options and write your answer below:

11 (1110) 10, 17 (172) 2, 13 (?) 5

A. 132
B. 135
C. 65
D. 133
E. 57

Answer:

12) In each set of numbers, the number in the brackets is related to the two numbers either side of it. Find this relation to work out the missing number '(?)' in the third set. Choose one of the option and write your answer below:

7 (35) 5, 8 (64) 8, 4 (?) 8

A. 14
B. 18
C. 32
D. 25
E. 23

Answer:

13) A four letter word is hidden between two words in the sentence below. These two words are always next to each other, but there may be punctuation between them. Find this four letter word from one of the options. Write your answer below:

"Are you feeling better?" he asked gently.

A. are you
B. asked gently
C. feeling better
D. he asked
E. you feeling

Answer:

14) A four letter word is hidden between two words in the sentence below. These two words are always next to each other, but there may be punctuation between them. Find this four letter word from one of the options. Write your answer below:

"Are you the father of Master Gibbons?" asked the headmaster, entering his office.

A. asked the
B. the father
C. headmaster entering
D. master gibbons
E. of master

Answer:

15) Choose the correct answer for the following problem. Write your answer below:

Jack takes a number, multiplies it by 3 and subtracts 7, giving an answer of 29. What was the number?

A. 10
B. 11
C. 12
D. 13
E. 14

Answer:

16) Choose the correct answer for the following problem. Write your answer below:

Maureen and Jay go for dinner together and spend £47.50 in total. There was a service charge of £5.15 and Maureen's meal cost £20.25. How much did Jay's meal cost?

A. £22.10
B. £19.60
C. £24.70
D. £21.50
E. £23.40

Answer:

17) Read the information provided and choose the single best answer for the question. Write your answer below:

Tia, Larry, Zain, Ben and Niall are discussing what flavours of ice cream they like. Larry and Zain are the only ones who like chocolate. Zain, Ben and Tia are the only ones who like vanilla. Tia, Larry and Ben are the only ones who like strawberry. Niall, Larry and Tia are the only ones who like mint.

Who only likes chocolate and vanilla flavour?

A. Tia
B. Larry
C. Zain
D. Ben
E. Niall

Answer:

18) Read the information provided and choose the single best answer for the question. Write your answer below:

Tia, Larry, Zain, Ben and Niall are discussing what flavours of ice cream they like. Larry and Zain are the only ones who like chocolate. Zain, Ben and Tia are the only ones who like vanilla. Larry and Ben are the only ones who like strawberry. Niall, Larry and Tia are the only ones who like mint.

Who only likes vanilla and mint?

A. Tia
B. Larry
C. Zain
D. Ben
E. Niall

Answer:

19) Select the word from the brackets that will complete the sentence in the most sensible way. Write your answer below:

Bird is to NEST as rabbit is to (home, field, burrow)

Answer:

20) Find one word from each group that together makes one correctly spelt word. The letters must not be rearranged. The word from the first group must always be used first. Write your answer below:

(lizard, snake, dragon) (fly, move, sail)

A. Lizardfly
B. Snakesail
C. Dragonsail
D. Dragonfly
E. Snakemove

Answer:

Verbal Reasoning - Test 30

Marks

21) Find the pair of letters that will continue the series. The alphabet is provided below to help you. Write your answer below:

A B C D E F G H I J K L M N O P Q R S T U V W X Y Z

KI, IK, GM, EO, CQ, ___?

Answer:

22) Select the two words inside the brackets that are connected in some way to the words outside the brackets. Write your answer below:

UNCLE MOTHER (friend, sister, doctor, plumber, father, dog, electrician)

Answer:

23) Select the word from the brackets that will complete the sentence in the most sensible way. Write your answer below:

Butcher is to MEAT as Greengrocer is to (bread, vegetables, laundry)

Answer:

24) Find the pair of letters that will complete the sentence in the best way. The alphabet is provided below to help you. Write your answer below:

A B C D E F G H I J K L M N O P Q R S T U V W X Y Z

LV is to JX as DT is to ___?

Answer:

25) You are required to move one letter from the first word to the second word, creating two new words. Use this to complete the sentence below.

NOTE GO

He tried _____ to let his _____ get the better of him.

Answer:

26) Write the letter that will complete the word in front of the brackets and begin the word after the brackets. The SAME letter must fit into BOTH sets of brackets. Write your answer below:

lam (_) ear, tom (_) est

Answer:

27) Select the two words inside the brackets that are connected in some way to the words outside the brackets. Write your answer below:

BOAT RAFT (car, ship, canoe, train, bus)

Answer:

28) Find the pair of letters that will complete the sentence in the best way. The alphabet is provided below to help you. Write your answer below:

A B C D E F G H I J K L M N O P Q R S T U V W X Y Z

WH is to XJ as MA is to ___?

Answer:

29) Select the pair of words, one from each group that are most opposite in meaning to each other from the options given below. Write your answer below:

(Fear Throw Harsh) (End Bravery Fight)

A. Fear Fight
B. Fear Bravery
C. Throw Fight
D. Harsh Bravery
E. Harsh Fight

Answer:

30) Choose the correct answer by completing the following functions and sums with the correct numbers and signs as appropriate. Write your answer below:

69 ÷ (5 − 2) + ___ = 2 × 16 − 4

A. 4
B. 5
C. 6
D. 7
E. 8

Answer:

Verbal Reasoning - Test 30

31) The words in brackets are formed from the main word. Identify the pattern to work out the missing word from the options given. Write your answer below:

Tetanus (sun), badminton (not), borrowed (?)

A. RED
B. DEW
C. ROB
D. WED
E. ROW

Answer:

32) Three consecutive letters are removed from the word in CAPITALS. These letters make a word. From the options, find the missing letters to complete the sentence. Write your answer below:

James marked his progress on the CHS.

A. ARM
B. ACE
C. AND
D. ANT
E. ART

Answer:

33) Find the number that best complete the series. Fill in the missing blank with one of the following options and write your answer below:

9, 27, __ , 63, 81

A. 45
B. 54
C. 36
D. 49
E. 51

Answer:

34) Three consecutive letters have been taken out of a word. Select which three letters have been omitted from the options. Write your answer below:

S___D

A. PAN
B. PAT
C. PEN
D. PEA
E. PAW

Answer:

35) You are required to move one letter from the first word to the second word, creating two new words. Write your answer below:

SOAK CAT.

Answer:

36) Write the letter that will complete the word in front of the brackets and begin the word after the brackets. The SAME letter must fit into BOTH sets of brackets. Write your answer below:

mos (_) ack, pas (_) ilk

Answer:

37) Select the pair of words, one from each group that are most opposite in meaning to each other from the options given. Write your answer below:

The opposite of (Check Tin Finish) is (Start Choose Follow).

A. Check Choose
B. Tin Follow
C. Finish Choose
D. Check Follow
E. Finish Start

Answer:

38) Select the TWO odd words from the options given. Write your answer below:

Glove, hand, arm, leg, trousers

A. Glove, hand
B. Hand arm
C. Leg trousers
D. Glove trousers
E. Arm leg

Answer:

39) Find the number that best complete the series. Fill in the missing blank with one of the following options and write your answer below:

28, 42, 56, __, 84

A. 66
B. 72
C. 58
D. 80
E. 70

Answer:

40) Three consecutive letters have been taken out of a word. Select which three letters have been omitted from the options. Write your answer below:

The girl kept playing one song on RE___T.

A. PAW
B. PAT
C. PAN
D. PEA
E. PEN

Answer:

Answers - Tests 16-30

Answer keys for all of the tests in this book

Instructions for Usage:

> Once you have completed a test, find the answers and mark the script.
> Each question is worth 1 mark, making a total score of 40.
> Review incorrect answers using the walkthrough for guidance.
> To monitor progress, use the progress chart and error tally table.

Mark Schemes

Test 16	Test 17	Test 18	Test 19	Test 20
1) D	1) C	1) 7	1) D	1) T
2) STEAM STROKE	2) ONE BREAD	2) P	2) D	2) Spider, ant
3) E	3) E	3) DG	3) C	3) GO
4) Turtle, iguana	4) Squash, cricket	4) D	4) E	4) JQ
5) TQ	5) C	5) C	5) C	5) A
6) A	6) A	6) A	6) C	6) E
7) D	7) C	7) C	7) Rabbit, mouse	7) C
8) E	8) C	8) C	8) HEN	8) C
9) C	9) C	9) E	9) BBQ	9) CEASE STRING
10) A	10) B	10) E	10) LPAJKF	10) Sad
11) E	11) A	11) B	11) 9	11) E
12) A	12) B	12) C	12) 15	12) E
13) D	13) B	13) A	13) T	13) C
14) B	14) QD	14) C	14) SPAIN	14) B
15) XY	15) KP	15) HUT SNIP	15) A	15) D
16) B	16) 8	16) Yellow, green	16) E	16) E
17) D	17) 14	17) Kid	17) C	17) Cook
18) C	18) R	18) YE	18) C	18) C
19) B	19) Dishwasher, toaster	19) B	19) A	19) KC
20) A	20) B	20) C	20) C	20) HB
21) B	21) BOW PART	21) C	21) D	21) D
22) E	22) QCZPVHZDV	22) B	22) OQ	22) E
23) Skirt	23) TRIANGLE	23) D	23) Kilogram, ounce	23) SAKE ARCH
24) D	24) B	24) A	24) E	24) OINOD
25) CS	25) NE	25) CAN SEND (CAN ENDS)	25) QY	25) BAGS
26) 9	26) BJ	26) HEXAGON	26) D	26) 9
27) 8	27) A	27) CUBE	27) A	27) 9
28) L	28) E	28) 11	28) E	28) S
29) Goldfish, catfish	29) B	29) B	29) C	29) Lamb, turkey
30) Read	30) B	30) Table, chair	30) A	30) D
31) HL	31) E	31) Foal	31) B	31) B
32) B	32) C	32) C	32) D	32) A
33) A	33) E	33) D	33) A	33) E
34) E	34) Kitchen	34) LB	34) TRAY SLOWLY	34) E
35) B	35) B	35) RK	35) S	35) D
36) E	36) E	36) B	36) SL	36) B
37) APE CHARM	37) C	37) E	37) MT	37) A
38) NTXH	38) D	38) C	38) B	38) E
39) RORWMY	39) A	39) B	39) D	39) C
40) C	40) Reptile	40) B	40) PLACE SAID	40) D

Verbal Reasoning

Mark Schemes

Test 21	Test 22	Test 23	Test 24	Test 25
1) D	1) 5	1) BAND TRICK	1) SOIL	1) E
2) D	2) 8	2) HSBTT	2) LEAVES	2) Tennis, squash
3) A	3) B	3) TULIP	3) 0	3) C
4) D	4) FW	4) E	4) 0	4) QA
5) D	5) A	5) ZJ	5) P	5) D
6) B	6) B	6) E	6) B	6) C
7) CO	7) E	7) D	7) A	7) B
8) FH	8) B	8) A	8) A	8) E
9) CONCEALER	9) A6X6	9) E	9) C	9) A
10) EYEBROWS	10) A	10) AJ	10) B	10) D
11) 1	11) E	11) E	11) B	11) B
12) 7	12) WX	12) Lamb, kid	12) C	12) D
13) K	13) D	13) Speaker	13) Hot	13) 16
14) B	14) E	14) E	14) D	14) 14
15) B	15) C	15) A	15) B	15) G (D)
16) C	16) E	16) B	16) B	16) Touch, smell
17) A	17) D	17) B	17) B	17) E
18) D	18) B	18) A	18) A	18) NG
19) Apple, plum	19) D	19) D	19) D	19) FO
20) Weight	20) Spoon, plate	20) B	20) D	20) D
21) C	21) GMPXFS	21) C	21) C	21) A
22) E	22) USFF	22) HOSE STRAND	22) ACE RATE	22) SUM CROOK
23) D	23) Ocean, stream	23) 6	23) T	23) JMEIGW
24) A	24) D	24) N	24) Apartment, bungalow	24) EPKAMCV
25) A	25) PATENT RAIN	25) B	25) FR	25) Sail
26) SAD NICE	26) Ground	26) EG	26) GH	26) E
27) G	27) D	27) D	27) E	27) E
28) Chair, stool	28) D	28) Distance	28) B	28) A
29) Drink	29) C	29) YD	29) C	29) B
30) B	30) B	30) E	30) D	30) E
31) HAM RANT	31) C	31) D	31) ROUND ROAD	31) E
32) C	32) D	32) E	32) Vulture, hawk	32) C
33) D	33) D	33) C	33) Pitch	33) OWN STAKE (TOW SNAKE)
34) A	34) C	34) B	34) C	34) Work
35) E	35) A	35) 10	35) OL	35) D
36) A	36) CAB CRANE	36) E	36) E	36) IB
37) C	37) Dinner	37) Shorts, shoes	37) B	37) A
38) MF	38) A	38) B	38) LU	38) B
39) NV	39) LM	39) D	39) E	39) C
40) B	40) E	40) D	40) E	40) B

Verbal Reasoning

Mark Schemes

Test 26	Test 27	Test 28	Test 29	Test 30
1) E	1) B	1) WRH	1) C	1) FOOT
2) E	2) HEAR DETER	2) KDQG	2) CAN UNITE	2) THUMB
3) C	3) A	3) A	3) IDFH	3) c
4) E	4) B	4) West	4) EAR	4) c
5) SOLDER GRAIN	5) Bakery	5) A	5) e	5) C
6) HMQRDYNJ	6) C	6) E	6) b	6) IT
7) JUDO	7) AB	7) D	7) B	7) B
8) D	8) E	8) E	8) PF	8) A
9) E	9) C	9) C	9) D	9) E
10) L	10) C	10) B	10) E	10) B
11) D	11) A	11) UY	11) C	11) B
12) TEN THANK	12) D	12) A	12) D	12) C
13) NA	13) A	13) D	13) E	13) B
14) A	14) KK	14) B	14) D	14) C
15) D	15) A	15) A	15) E	15) C
16) E	16) D	16) C	16) C	16) A
17) A	17) T	17) B	17) D	17) C
18) A	18) Cat, dog	18) E	18) D	18) A
19) E	19) A	19) B	19) Venus, Saturn	19) Burrow
20) A	20) HER DRAFT	20) E	20) Subtract	20) D
21) B	21) LACROSSE	21) E	21) A	21) AS
22) C	22) RUGBY	22) D	22) HOSE CART	22) Sister, father
23) S (T)	23) H	23) D	23) M	23) Vegetables
24) Fox, lion	24) Lorry, van	24) M	24) Sunglasses	24) BV
25) B	25) A	25) E	25) E	25) NOT EGO
26) YW	26) HV	26) REED BEGAN	26) DY	26) B
27) A	27) B	27) Beetle, cockroach	27) E	27) Ship, canoe
28) B	28) B	28) Bird	28) A	28) NC
29) E	29) C	29) KF	29) C	29) B
30) C	30) A	30) A	30) E	30) B
31) D	31) D	31) C	31) B	31) B
32) B	32) A	32) A	32) C	32) E
33) Month	33) D	33) E	33) A	33) A
34) C	34) Court	34) B	34) A	34) C
35) WB	35) LO	35) TO READY	35) A	35) OAK CAST (OAK CATS)
36) UN	36) B	36) F	36) P (D)	36) S
37) A	37) C	37) Carrots, broccoli	37) Hospital, bank	37) E
38) A	38) C	38) OR	38) GM	38) D
39) Jog, row	39) C	39) QH	39) D	39) E
40) Milk	40) D	40) A	40) LF	40) D

Verbal Reasoning

Progress Chart

Progress Chart

After marking each Verbal Reasoning test, find where your child's test score meets the upwards arrow of the corresponding test, and draw a cross. You can find out what estimated percentage of candidates would achieve a lower score by reading off the percentile values to the right for each test. To better spot the trend of how your child is progressing in terms of test scores and percentiles, connect successive crosses with straight lines. Underneath the chart, you can write down the scores and percentiles successively so that you can quickly look back on them later.

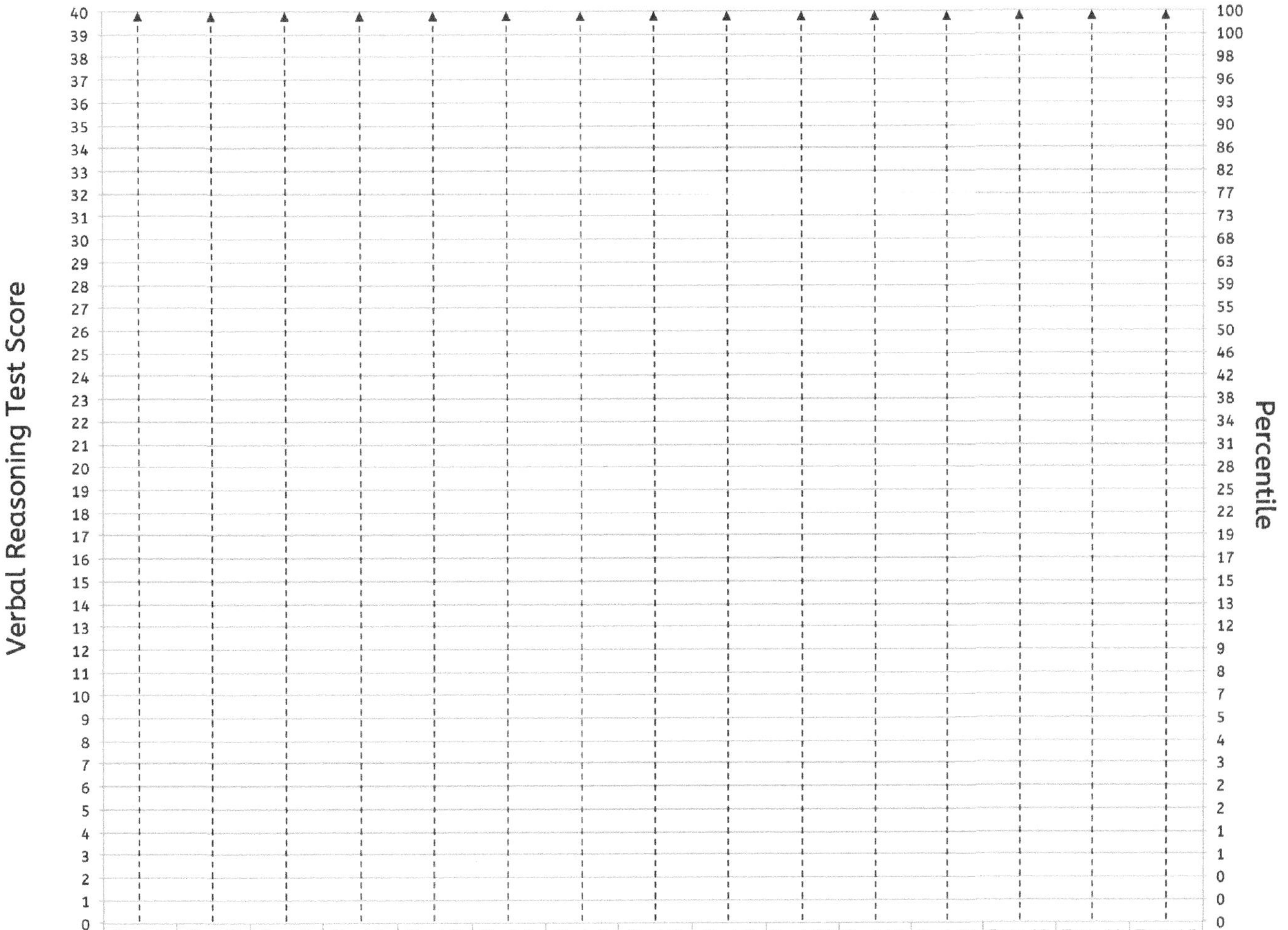

	Test 1	Test 2	Test 3	Test 4	Test 5	Test 6	Test 7	Test 8	Test 9	Test 10	Test 11	Test 12	Test 13	Test 14	Test 15
Score															
Percentile															

To understand and better categorise the progress charts, you can take the data and put it into the performance analysis chart on the next page. This chart allows you to develop a grading system to better study the scores that your child is getting.

We understand the value of being able to closely record and monitor your child's progress - indeed, many parents build rewards systems around them to help get their children into a steady work ethic. However, it is important that your child does not get disheartened if they do not score the mark they wanted. It is likely that as they become more familiar with the syllabus, they will achieve higher and higher marks. The purpose of this chart is for you to understand what rough level your child is at now, and to build targets around it.

On the contrary, if your child is scoring very highly, then these progress charts should provide some strong reassurance. It is important that your child keeps working through the tests to ensure that their level doesn't drop. Moreover, you may want to start thinking about scholarship programmes and raising your child's targets in accordance with these. We have intentionally included some scholarship-standard questions in every test that are of very high difficulty. It is therefore extremely uncommon that a child scores 100% in a test. We like to make sure that our papers push candidates at every level.

To build these charts, we ran trial tests around the UK and accumulated data from several students who were all due to sit independent school exams within the next 12 months. We corresponded the different scores that students were getting to the percentile that they fell within. It is important to note that while your child's scores climb, the percentile increase will follow a different pattern. Gaining 5 marks with a baseline score of 20/40 corresponds to a percentile climb of 18%, whereas with a baseline score of 35/40 the percentile climb is only 10%. It becomes harder and harder to climb those last few percentiles!

Performance Analysis

Performance Analysis Graphs and Grading

Use the graphs to analyse your child's performance. Simply take their score in any test, and read off the percentile to find out how your child did compared to others. Please note that since our tests vary in difficultly slightly, and since these graphs are estimates across all of our tests, you should take slight changes in performance lightly. It is possible for you to read off the percentiles using the progress chart on the previous page alone, but this graph makes it more clear visually how student scores are spread out. The table below the graph explains how you can grade each paper, and is colour co-ordinated with the graph.

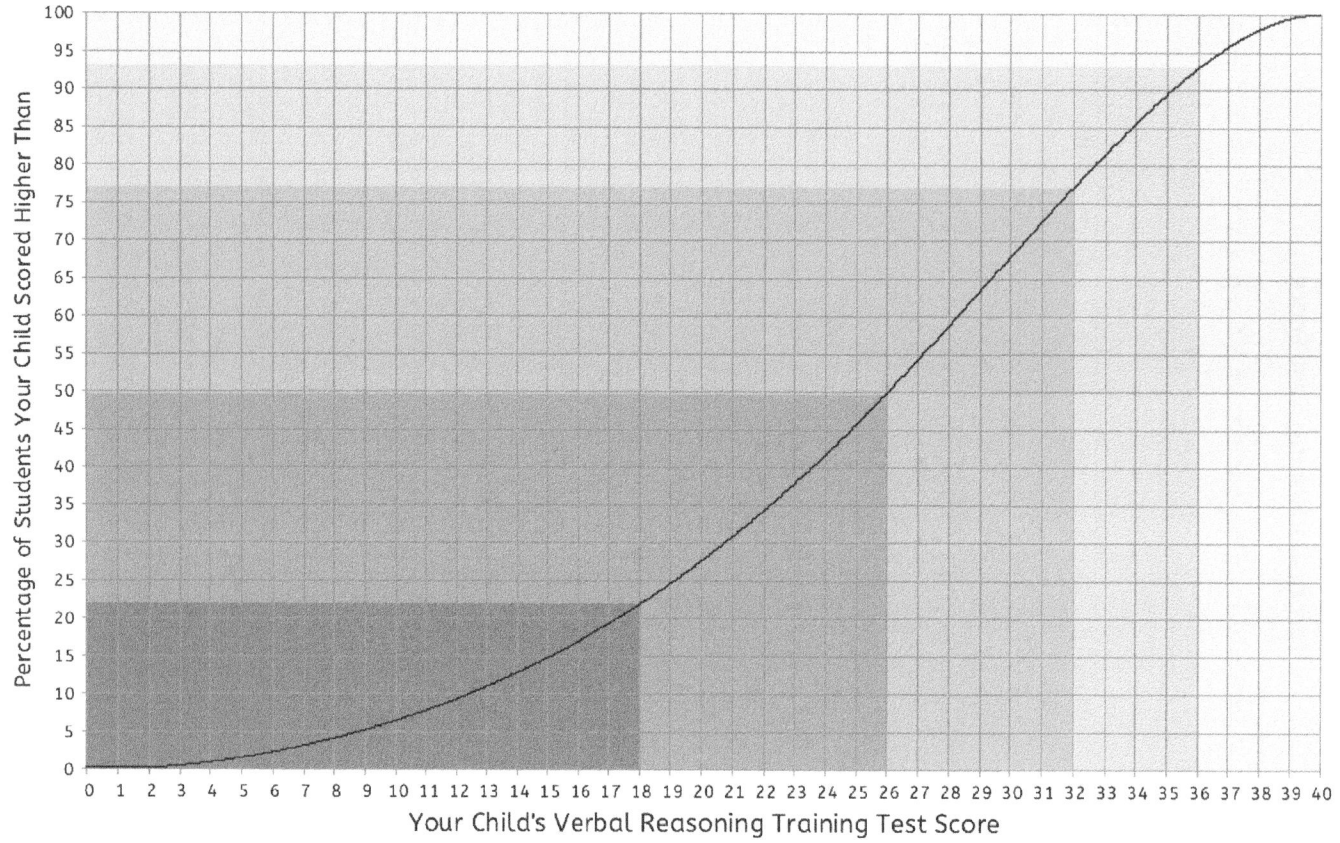

Verbal Reasoning Score	Grade
37-40	Outstanding
33-36	Excellent
27-32	Satisfactory
19-26	Coasting
0-18	Improvement Needed

Students usually need a small amount of time to adapt to different Verbal Reasoning question types, after which performance improves. Our syllabus is diverse and we have written questions from every angle to keep your child on their toes.

While sitting these papers, children should try and find methods for each individual question type that work for them. Shortcuts and tricks are easy to find, but the ones your child should use are the ones that are suited to their style of learning.

You may find this grading system useful in building up more specific reward systems for your child. Please remember that this data was collected from a large number of students who were within 12 months of sitting their Independent School 11+ examinations. We understand that some parents give their children our resources a little early, in order to get ahead of the rest of the cohort. In these contexts, the grading system may be less appropriate for them. The person who knows your child the best is you, and if these targets don't work for you, then we recommend that you change them to suit your needs.

If your child is scoring 0-18, we recommend strongly that you cover content with them before they attempt further tests. It means that there is a good chance that they are not ready to sit the tests just yet - sitting repeated tests in such a case will not build up their knowledge of first principles. At Secondary Entrance, we offer a holistic set of services, and so if you feel that your child needs help with learning the concepts, please feel free to turn to our In-Person and Skype tuition services.

If your child is scoring 37-40, their mark is outstanding. This means that they are performing extremely highly and you may want to begin thinking about scholarship training. Again, our In-Person and Skype tuition services can help you with this if you wish.

Tally Table

Tally Table

After marking each Verbal Reasoning test, you can refer back to the sample paper walkthrough and see which types of question your child is getting wrong. You can tally these errors here, and figure out which areas they need to work on the most.

	TEST 1	TEST 2	TEST 3	TEST 4	TEST 5	TEST 6	TEST 7	TEST 8	TEST 9	TEST 10	TEST 11	TEST 12	TEST 13	TEST 14	TEST 15	TOTAL
REMOVING SUBSET WORDS																
DECIPHERING WORDS																
REARRANGED WORDS																
INCOMPLETE WORDS																
COMBINING WORDS																
COMMON WORD ASSOCIATIONS																
ALPHABET CODES																
ALPHABET PUZZLES																
NUMBER CODES																
WORD RELATIONS																
SIMILES																
LETTER SEQUENCES																
NUMBER SEQUENCES																
OPPOSITES																
DIFFERENTIATING WORDS																
VERBAL MATHS PROBLEMS																
PRACTICAL MATHS PROBLEMS																
FUNCTIONS																
ALGEBRAIC EQUATIONS																
HIDDEN WORDS																

Some children are very ordered and logical, whereas others have their strengths in spatial problem solving or in retaining information. These differences mean that every student has a particular set of question styles which they find the most hardest.

It is only healthy for a child to work a limited number of hours in a day and, especially considering this in the run up to the exam, working smart is critical. This table helps you and your child to understand where the most scope is to gain marks quickly.

Healthy Learning Tips

Healthy Learning Tips

11+ revision can get intense, particularly when close to the exams. It is crucial to supplement learning with a routine that consists of sufficient exercise, outdoor activity, proper diet and ample sleep, in order to stay efficient and healthy.

Can Work Become a Hobby?

How to revise without sitting at a desk

At Secondary Entrance, we truly believe in the term 'work hard play hard'. We wouldn't want your child to sit and revise abstract concepts without understanding the real life context. Sometimes it is not completely clear to a child why they may be working so hard on 11+ test papers and revising. Often it is in their benefit that they do not, to avoid unnecessary stress nearer to an exam. As an 11+ parent, being immersed within the learning process as much as your child is fundamental to their learning.

Foster a love for learning

Doing 11+ practice papers can be boring. We know because we ourselves remember all those years ago revising for our very own 11+ exams, and wanted to play outside or watch TV, not sit at a desk and do past papers. However, learning is at its best when you or your child are not aware of it, or better yet, when you are both enjoying it. By providing a learning environment that is ever-changing and engaging, learning can move outside of answering questions. Examples of this include going into the garden and counting flowers or spotting animals.

How can I Create a Structured and Varied Learning Environment?

Have something to look forward to, every time

When your child is about to start a paper, give them something to look forward to once they complete it, such as a snack, or time playing their favourite game. Having this ensures that work is not associated with unhappy thoughts, and instead is a journey, with a prize at the end of it.

Spread out the learning process in small, bite-sized chunks

A child's brain is amazing! It is able to absorb vast amount of information, more so than adults, and can learn at a very rapid rate. However, this rapid level of learning also requires regular breaks and plenty of nourishment. It is unrealistic to expect your child to work for more than an hour at a time. Create big breaks in between tests, to allow their brains lots of time to consolidate their learning.

Take learning outside of the study room!

Try going to the local park or museum! Challenge your child in new ways, such as creating maths problems using sticks or stones in the park. By making learning an engaging activity, children are more likely to retain information and are less likely to avoid working. Topics like non-verbal reasoning simply require pattern recognition, therefore spotting patterns in the environment is still learning but in a less obvious way than direct mathematics, for example. Being active within the learning process as a parent gives a child further reason to want to work. They go through this as part of a team. Leading by example is an effective means of teaching healthy learning habits.

Physical exercise is just as important as mental exercise!

It is vital that whilst you exercise your mind, you also exercise your body. Ensuring your child engages in activity every day is so important to their well-being, and also ensures that they feel fresh and energised when they do work. Whether this is swimming, running, playing in the park or football, exercise of any sort is as important as working!

Sleep!

Whilst your child works during the day, it is also important to avoid working too late at night, and that they have at least 8 hours of sleep a night. Sleep is such a valuable part of the revision process, helping the brain to filter through the information of the day, build new connections and organise it for quick retrieval at a later date. A child that is well rested will get more from a revision session than one that is sleep deprived, thus this should not be overlooked.

Verbal Reasoning

Healthy Learning Tips

How can I Improve my Child's Learning Outside of School?

Going to museums

Museums are a brilliant way of bringing science, history and the arts to life. They have a lot of fun interactive exhibits to keep children entertained, but to also educate them on the fundamentals of science and art. By seeing important artefacts and demonstrations, children begin to understand the real-life applications of what they have studied.

Shopping with your child

Whilst this may simply be grocery shopping, getting them to calculate the price of the items in your basket is great for mental maths and can make any shopping trip exciting! You could also ask them to work out the price of a product after a discount, or how much you could save in your basket with 2 for 1 deals considered.

Travelling

Perhaps your child could assist you in planning a route, or finding the fastest way of getting around town. Giving them real world problems with an incentive is fun and engaging, and helps develop problem solving abilities! If in London they could plan a tube route, or if in a car they could work out how long it will take to get to your destination if you give them the distance and speed you are travelling at.

Spelling games whilst reading the newspaper

Newspapers are a great place to find fun little puzzles, such as crosswords and Sudokus. You may also be able to find a number of new words that your child has never encountered before, and be able to teach them what they mean in the process. Moreover, secondary schools that interview often like to ask about what your child may have seen in the news, and so you can keep them current on events that are happening in the world.

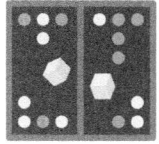

Playing board games such as Pictionary or Scrabble!

Scrabble is an effective means of improving a child's vocabulary in a relaxed and fun environment! It challenges them to sift through all their current vocabulary, but also to run to the dictionary to find new words! They will continually question whether certain combinations of letters make a word or not. This truly is verbal reasoning in action! Pictionary improves their visual and perceptive skills, and so may indirectly help them with maths and non-verbal reasoning. It does so in a fun way where the emphasis is on drawing and earning points.

Ultimately, Learning Should be Fun

Try to find learning resources that your child enjoys using

Whilst at Secondary Entrance we want your child to achieve the best they possibly can, it must be remembered that they are still developing socially, physically and mentally. Giving them the widest possible number of experiences and exposure to different activities is at the core of fostering life-long learning. For them to develop their own reasoning of situations is the ultimate goal of all of our papers. Our aim has been to design our resources in a way that provides long-term as well as short-term benefits to your child. We welcome any feedback about your own personal thoughts on education, as we too are also learning, and want to offer the best possible products to our clients!

11+ Exam Preparation Advice

How to Prepare for the 11+ Exams

At Secondary Entrance, we have all done exams. A lot of them. The majority of our staff are continually being assessed even now, and so our understanding of exams goes far beyond just being academically prepared for them.

12 months before the exam:

You and your child should familiarise yourself with the exam style for whichever exam your child will be sitting. You should try and find the appropriate syllabuses if they exist, or look at existing materials on the school's website to get a general idea of what is tested.

It is also worth keeping an eye on how your child is doing at school at this stage, and try to develop a good idea of their strengths and weaknesses. With this knowledge, you should aim to fill out any gaps in their knowledge. How can Secondary Entrance help? Within each of our 11+ practice papers, a large range of syllabus points are accounted for. In this way, you can identify the knowledge gaps early on and work smart.

Your child should attempt practice papers to get used to doing exams. This should be in a non-pressured environment, with plenty of time to read, internalise and ponder over every question. They should do no more than one paper a day, and should rotate papers to keep it mixed.

6 months before the exam:

Your child should be quite well rehearsed with the idea of taking practice papers in a relaxed environment by this stage. You may now attempt to time the papers, as per the recommendations at the front of the practice packs.

It may be that your child does not finish the paper, or that they rush near the end and miss some easy marks. These sorts of mistakes are important to make, as they will teach your child exam technique. They will learn naturally that missing out long-winded questions and revisiting them later may make sense if they are only worth one mark. Remember that getting your child into the habit of doing timed papers reduces stress closer to the exam, as they are familiar with what they will ultimately have to do.

3 months before the exam:

The number of papers your child is doing can increase up to a maximum of 2-3 per day at this point. Their timing should now be more up to speed, and you can experiment with targets to help them increase their marks further if you find that they are starting to plateau.

If your child starts to tire, or begins to adopt rout learning routines, this is often an indication that things need to be mixed up a little bit. Visit our healthy learning advice to see the variety of learning approaches that you may wish to try out.

1 month before the exam:

11+ exam technique is now the focus. It may help, even if only for a short period of time, to recruit a tutor who can run through technique tips with your child. A tutor can also help at this stage with topics which are proving to be a persistent problem.

The other benefit that having a tutor or otherwise constantly working with your child can have is taking care of nerves. With such little time coming up to the exam, it is normal for some panic to surface. Having a tutor can help reassure you that a professional is taking care of your child's immediate academic needs.

1 week before the exam:

At this point, most of the preparation for the 11+ should be complete, and most of your Secondary Entrance papers should be completed. Some final practice using past papers that the schools may offer on their website may help keep your child's mind freshly targeted to the specific material that they are about to encounter.

You must remember that most of the preparation at this point is complete, and that rest and leisure remain very important. Cramming hundreds of papers into this week is not an effective means of preparation, and leads to anxiety and fatigue.

The day of the exam:

All the preparation is now complete. You and your child are as prepared as they ever could be for the 11+ exam papers, and your child should have nothing to worry about. They should know what to expect for the exam, and if there is a question that they cannot do, they have adequate preparation to keep them calm and help them have as good a shot as possible.

With the help of adequate advice, tutoring and high quality preparation material, hopefully Secondary Entrance has been able to unload much of the stress for both you and your child.

Revision Timetables

Revision Timetables

A little a day goes a long way. Equally, it is important for your child not to wear themselves out by working too hard, too soon. Our revision schedules are sensible, effective and integrate healthy supplements to your child's learning.

12 Months Before the Exams

We recommend this schedule for those with a year to go before their exam - it is not too intense at all. It covers three tests in a week, and 'break-days' have a single slot to mark the previous day's paper and go over any incorrect answers.

Monday	Tuesday	Wednesday	Thursday	Friday	Saturday	Sunday
Day 1 Maths - Test 1: 60 Minutes	**Day 2** Maths - Review: 25 Minutes	**Day 3** English - Test 1: 70 Minutes	**Day 4** English - Review: 25 Minutes	**Day 5** Verbal - Test 1: 40 Minutes	**Day 6** Verbal - Review: 25 Minutes	**Day 7** Break: Full Day
Day 8 Non-Verbal - Test 1: 60 Minutes	**Day 9** Non-Verbal - Review: 25 Minutes	**Day 10** Maths - Test 2: 60 Minutes	**Day 11** Maths - Review: 25 Minutes	**Day 12** English - Test 2: 70 Minutes	**Day 13** English - Review: 25 Minutes	**Day 14** Break: Full Day
Day 15 Verbal - Test 2: 40 Minutes	**Day 16** Verbal - Review: 25 Minutes	**Day 17** Non-Verbal - Test 2: 60 Minutes	**Day 18** Non-Verbal - Review: 25 Minutes	**Day 19** Maths - Test 3: 60 Minutes	**Day 20** Maths - Review: 25 Minutes	**Day 21** Break: Full Day
Day 22 English - Test 3: 70 Minutes	**Day 23** English - Review: 25 Minutes	**Day 24** Verbal - Test 3: 40 Minutes	**Day 25** Verbal - Review: 25 Minutes	**Day 26** Non-Verbal - Test 3: 60 Minutes	**Day 27** Non-Verbal - Review: 25 Minutes	**Day 28** Break: Full Day
Day 29 Maths - Test 4: 60 Minutes	**Day 30** Maths - Review: 25 Minutes	**Day 31** English - Test 4: 70 Minutes	And So On...			

The 31-Day Revision Challenge

Finding a good revision routine is difficult, and your child will need to do preparation on top of training tests. This schedule slowly increases the amount of daily work done on three preparatory activities: mental maths, spelling and book reading.

Monday	Tuesday	Wednesday	Thursday	Friday	Saturday	Sunday
Day 1 Mental Maths: 10 Minutes	**Day 2** Spelling Work: 10 Minutes	**Day 3** Read a Book: 10 Minutes	**Day 4** Break: Full Evening	**Day 5** Mental Maths: 15 Minutes	**Day 6** Spelling Work: 15 Minutes	**Day 7** Read a Book: 15 Minutes
Day 8 Break: Full Evening	**Day 9** Mental Maths: 20 Minutes	**Day 10** Spelling Work: 20 Minutes	**Day 11** Read a Book: 20 Minutes	**Day 12** Break: Full Evening	**Day 13** Mental Maths: 30 Minutes	**Day 14** Spelling Work: 30 Minutes
Day 15 Read a Book: 30 Minutes	**Day 16** Break: Full Evening	**Day 17** Mental Maths: 35 Minutes	**Day 18** Spelling Work: 35 Minutes	**Day 19** Read a Book: 35 Minutes	**Day 20** Break: Full Evening	**Day 21** Mental Maths: 40 Minutes
Day 22 Spelling Work: 40 Minutes	**Day 23** Read a Book: 40 Minutes	**Day 24** Break: Full Evening	**Day 25** Mental Maths: 45 Minutes	**Day 26** Spelling Work: 45 Minutes	**Day 27** Read a Book: 45 Minutes	**Day 28** Break: Full Evening
Day 29 Mental Maths: 50 Minutes	**Day 30** Spelling Work: 50 Minutes	**Day 31** Read a Book: 50 Minutes				

Revision Timetables

<u>In the Run-Up: Intense Learning</u>

It is crucial that your child does not experience burn-out, however in the final weeks their preparation will increase. They should never sit more than two tests in a day, and our routine demonstrates the healthy way to handle the final stretch.

Time:	Monday	Tuesday	Wednesday	Thursday	Friday	Saturday	Sunday
8:00am - 9:00am	Wake up, eat breakfast, and get ready for the day!						
9:00am - 10:00am	Maths - Test 1: 60 Minutes	VR - Test 1: 40 Minutes	English - Test 2: 70 Minutes	NVR - Test 2: 60 Minutes	Maths - Test 3: 60 Minutes	VR - Test 3: 40 Minutes	NVR - Test 3: 60 Minutes
10:00am - 11:00am	Read a Book	Break: Have a snack (some fruit)		Spelling Work	Break: Watch TV or play games		Mental Maths Work
11:00am - 12:00pm	Maths Review: 25 Minutes	VR Review: 25 Minutes	English Review: 25 Minutes	NVR Review: 25 Minutes	Maths Review: 25 Minutes	VR Review: 25 Minutes	NVR Review: 25 Minutes
12:00pm - 1:00pm	Lunch Break						
1:00pm - 2:00pm	English - Test 1: 70 Minutes	NVR - Test 1: 60 Minutes	Maths - Test 2: 60 Minutes	VR - Test 2: 40 Minutes	English - Test 3: 70 Minutes		
2:00pm - 3:00pm	Break: Play outside and be active					Break: Meet some friends or take part in some extracurricular activity	
3:00pm - 4:00pm	English Review: 25 Minutes	NVR Review: 25 Minutes	Maths Review: 25 Minutes	VR Review: 25 Minutes	English Review: 25 Minutes		

<u>Holiday Revision: Blank Timetable</u>

It goes without saying that you know your child best, and so you may wish to create your own custom timetable for your child to work through. The working hours are limited to between 8am and 4pm, as your child is used to school hours.

<u>Advice on Using our Timetables</u>

Time:	Monday	Tuesday	Wednesday	Thursday	Friday	Saturday	Sunday
8:00am - 9:00am							
9:00am - 10:00am							
10:00am - 11:00am							
11:00am - 12:00pm							
12:00pm - 1:00pm							
1:00pm - 2:00pm							
2:00pm - 3:00pm							
3:00pm - 4:00pm							

As much as we want to steer you in the right direction, we at Secondary Entrance acknowledge that every child is unique, and has their own, independent learning style. In accordance with this, we strongly encourage you to modify and adjust our timetables around your child's subject needs, extra-curricular activities and their social life.

Verbal Reasoning

That's the end of the book. What else do we offer?

We've got a three part education system, designed to get your child into their chosen school:

1. 11+ Practice Papers
240 outstanding quality tests for the 4 core subjects. We've scrutinised every question to ensure quality.

2. Tutoring Services
We offer in-person and online tutoring services. All of our tutors have attended world-leading universities.

3. 11+ Practice Papers
www.Independent11Plus.co.uk
We provide learning guides and supplementary material.

Meet our authors and editors
For verbal reasoning book 1 to book 4
Our authors have all attended Cambridge and Imperial – world-leading universities.

AUTHOR: Aaran Patel
MBBS: Imperial
BSc: Imperial
Studying: Medicine

AUTHOR: Russell de Sá
MBBS: Imperial
BSc: Imperial
Studying: Medicine

AUTHOR & EDITOR: Suraj Joshi
MBBS: Imperial
BSc: Imperial
Studying: Medicine

EDITOR: Aneesh Aggarwal
MBBS: Cambridge
BA: Cambridge
Studying: Medicine

EDITOR: Christiana Naziris
MSc: Cambridge
BA: Cambridge
Studied: Physics

References
Icons from www.flaticon.com

'Tree' icon made by Smashicons
'Books' icon made by Freepik
'Ping Pong' icon made by Freepik
'Apple' icon made by Freepik
'Landscape' icon made by Freepik
'Skipping Rope' icon made by Freepik
'Sleep' icon made by Freepik
'Museum' icon made by Freepik
'Grocery' icon made by Smashicons
'Sunbed' icon made by Smashicons
'Newspaper' icon made by Smashicons
'Backgammon' icon made by Nikita Golubev
'Baby' icon made by Freepik
'Calendar' icon made by Freepik
'Day and Night' icon made by Freepik
'Settings' icon made by Freepik
'Newton's Cradle' icon made by Freepik
'Time' icon made by Freepik
'Bar Chart' icon made by Freepik
'Goal' icon made by Freepik
'Time Management' icon made by Freepik
'Analytics' icon made by Freepik
All other graphics are either open source or produced by Secondary Entrance

Printed and bound by CPI Group (UK) Ltd, Croydon, CR0 4YY
05/01/2026
02029132-0001